6 00 112472 3
KU-204-649

SERBIAN POETRY AND MILUTIN BOJIĆ

MIHAILO DORDEVIĆ

UNIVERSITY LIBRARY
NOTTINGHAM

EAST EUROPEAN QUARTERLY, BOULDER
DISTRIBUTED BY COLUMBIA UNIVERSITY PRESS
NEW YORK

1977

EAST EUROPEAN MONOGRAPHS, NO. XXXIV

Mihailo Dordević is Professor of Humanities
and Comparative Literature
at The Pennsylvania State University

Copyright 1977 by East European Quarterly
Library of Congress Card Number 77-0000
ISBN 0-914710-27-3

Printed in the United States of America

For my brother Dimitrije Djordjević
and his grandchildren
Vladimir and Daniela Marković

TABLE OF CONTENTS

Foreword v

Serbian Poetry at the Beginning of the
Twentieth Century 1

Milutin Bojić, Biography 15

Milutin Bojić, Lyric Poet 27

Milutin Bojić, Epic and Dramatic Poet 52

Influences in Serbian Poetry 71

Milutin Bojić, Poems in Translation 83

Bibliography 97

Glossary 101

FOREWORD

The events of World War I and, subsequently, the formation of a Yugoslav state tended to remove Bojić, and others who had written primarily in the same period, from the mainstream of intellectual and artistic endeavor. Furthermore, Jovan Skerlić, the leading critic of the period, died before the poetic movement of which Bojić was a part could come to full flower. The works of Bojić, indeed, Serbian poetry and poets of the early twentieth century were neither explored nor analyzed in depth in the period that followed.

Because so few critical works have been written, the place of Milutin Bojić in Serbian literature has long remained undefined. The few articles that deal with his poetry are mainly eulogies or brief notes, mostly unsigned, which indicate only that Bojić acquired many friends during his brief life. The judgments of the literary critics of his time are both personal and contradictory, so much so that they cannot serve as the basis for a serious evaluation of his work. Obviously, therefore, there is a great need for an objective analysis of Bojić's poetry, a need this book hopes to meet.

No critic, no matter how biased, has ever attacked Bojić for his versification, a fact that shows the controversy over Bojić's poetry has to do with what he wrote, not how he wrote it. Those emotionally attuned to the subtleties of love or the evocative powers of symbolism can hardly be expected to appreciate a Victor Hugo or the romantic magnificence of Bojić. After all, bloodstains look ugly on the moirée silk of the symbolists, just as moirée silk looks ugly in times of national catastrophe. Those who believe the poetic Muse to be the pale and pensive girl who inspired the poet Jovan Dučić cannot understand a man such as Bojić, who was, as shown in his first youthful poems, an unleashed worshipper of Bacchus. Those who admire Albert Samain's *Infanta*, who dreams over wilted rose petals, may well fail to understand Bojić's Muse, who lives for a kiss in the sunshine, when "to part lips means to die." Many critics not only reject the essence of Bojić's lyricism, but also conclude that his negative qualities far outweight his positive qualities; they simply focus on the imbalance in a poetic work whose aim is to be romantically powerful rather than subtly harmonious.

A poem by Bojić never emulates the music of Scarlatti. It is a storm, the powerful and frightening roar of ice breaking in the spring, a sound expressing the strength of suddenly liberated torrents. Bojić's poems should therefore be read in one's youth, when the blood is in turmoil and when one turns to poetry seeking neither melancholy nor philosophy. If the youth of Serbia, and not elderly critics, wrote the history of Serbian poetry, Bojić would undoubtedly hold an important and even vital place in it. Their judgment would of course not be objective, but it would be no more subjective than the academic critics' condemnation of Bojić. Even if Bojić is not entitled to the lofty praise that youth would give him, he was certainly no minor poet. Though in his first works he was a purely lyric poet, he matured with time and wartime experiences into a visionary epic poet.

He may be a lesser poet than Milan Rakić and Jovan Dučić; he certainly ranks with Rajić, Dis and Pandurović, and he is much better than Svetislav Stefanović, Milutin Jelić and Milutin Jovanović.

It is hoped that this book will clarify and substantiate these statements.

I am indebted to Miss Radmila Todorović, Bojić's fiancée, for putting the poet's unpublished poems and correspondence at my disposal, as well as for the many hours of conversation that helped me gain a clearer understanding of the poet's personality. Without her help, this book would never have been written. I am also indebted to Professor Dimitirje Djordjević, of the University of California at Santa Barbara, for his invaluable advice on reorganizing the manuscript and bringing it to its final form. I am deeply grateful to Mrs. Jelisaveta Stanojevich-Allen, bibliographer at the Dunbarton Oaks Center for Byzantine Studies, Washington, D.C., who compiled the glossary to this book.

All the translations of Bojić's poems were done by the writer for the American reader with the hope that the lyrical spirit of the poet has not been altered too much. The verse contained in this book should contribute to a greater understanding of Serbian poetry at the beginning of the twentieth century, and the glossary should introduce the foreign reader to the cultural, social, and political climate of Serbia in Bojić's time.

SERBIAN POETRY AT THE BEGINNING OF THE TWENTIETH CENTURY

At the beginning of the twentieth century, Serbia was at last free of the centuries-old Turkish yoke. Its rulers and citizens spared no efforts to raise the status of the country from a nineteenth-century Balkan principality to a modern European kingdom. The resulting changes in social and economic life did not go without effect on the country's cultural life. New ideas sprang up in all fields of cultural endeavor, and the cultural and artistic milieu of Serbia changed drastically. In literature, more sophisticated aesthetic values found acceptance, and, in consequence, new literary forms began to appear.

The world of literature, in which Russian and German were heretofore dominant cultures, began to look more and more to France. There are two immediate reasons for this: first, a more modern, more sophisticated society was more likely to absorb French influences, and, second, more and more young men chose to study in France, rather than in Germany and Russia, as previous generations had done. Thus, the nineteenth-century realistic prose of Glišić, Ranković, and Sremac was gradually abandoned, and a new poetry, which was inspired by the Symbolist and Parnassian movements in France, took its place.

But France became the dominant cultural influence in Serbia not only because artistic concepts were evolving, but also because the most famous authors of nineteenth-century Serbia were dying out, almost as if they were leaving the literary scene to the new poets.[1] Thus, the new poets had to fill a void. They were called on not only to give expression to the new and more European cultural atmosphere, but also to develop it to its full potential. Skerlić well understood that the new poets were starting anew: "The authors of the nineteenth century, with all their differences nevertheless share a unity of literary ideas and concepts. Each of the young poets of the twentieth century had his own concepts and well-defined ideas. This phenomenon made it extremely difficult for the literary critic to label

---

[1] A brief survey of the authors who died at the beginning of the twentieth century gives an idea of the created void: Jovan Ilić in 1901, Zmaj-Jovan Jovanović in 1904, Božidar Knežević and Janko Veselinović in 1905, Stevan Sremac in 1906, Milorad Mitrović in 1907, Milovan Glišić, Sima Matavulj, and Radoje Domanović in 1908, and Laza Kostić in 1910.

new poetic achievements as specific schools, and place them in a continuation of the organized pattern that evolved from the romanticism of the 1860-1870 years, to the realism after 1870."[2] Thus, far more than new cultural influences were involved; a new generation stood on the threshold of a literary frontier.

In general culture, the natural sciences, which the generations of the nineteenth century had discovered and eagerly embraced, were losing ground rapidly. Russian realism was still a strong influence, although its adherents no longer imitated it beyond all sense of proportion. Its chaotic elements were now settling down within reasonable bounds, and realism was thus becoming more sober and solid. Neither were the new poets satisfied with the oversimplified spirit of the romantics. As social and cultural life in Serbia became more sophisticated, they began to see the need for a more elaborate versification. They became aware of the techniques required to polish a poem or other such work once the original inspiration had been jotted down. It must be pointed out that Serbia had still much to learn at the beginning of the century. It had to create fundamental and indispensable institutions, primarily in the judiciary and in health administration, as well as a system of organization patterned after that of the West. All this required young men who had been trained abroad.

Though young Serbs had already been trained abroad in the nineteenth century, this became more common in the first decade of the twentieth century. When these young men returned home, they brought with them literary ideas and aesthetic concepts they had acquired abroad. They began adapting European techniques to the needs of a young, vital country that was awakening after the long Turkish occupation. Seen from today, the development of Serbia at the beginning of the twentieth century seems prodigious, as it progressed in leaps and bounds over the centuries it had lost.

A striving for perfection became apparent, as was the need of the new generations to understand and respect the achievements of the West. The young were attracted to the university, and each year the courses offered were more and more heavily attended. The Bohemian life in Skadarlija[3] was over, as was the era of long-haired poets whose inspiration dwelled too often at the bottom of wine bottles. But it would be wrong to assume that the new poets were not

---

[2]Jovan Skerlić, *Istorija Srpske Književnosti*, Second Edition, Belgrade, 1921, p. 43.

[3]A part of Belgrade known as a gathering place for artists.

young. They had their own excesses, some of which are legendary. The difference was that they did not search for inspiration solely in their youthful excesses. They were no longer seen only in cafés, but more frequently at the university or in the National Library. Milutin Bojić spent long hours there, searching in ancient Serbian texts for expressions and poetic imagery that, though beautiful, had long been forgotten.

Certain courses, particularly those taught by Bogdan Popović and Brana Petronijević at the University, were overcrowded. The audience was made up not only of students, but also of a great number of young businessmen and merchants. This was something quite new, for in the previous century, culture had been restricted to a small number of intellectuals. In the twentieth century, Belgrade University became the meeting place for the new generation.

At the beginning of the century, Belgrade was shedding the remains of the small town it was under the Turkish occupation and was rapidly becoming a modern European city. It was also becoming the cultural center of the country, with a growing intellectual and artistic life of its own. This was especially evident in three poles of attraction: The university, the offices of the literary reviews, and the National Theater.

The founding of the literary review *Srpski Knježevni Glasnik* in 1901 can be considered as the dividing line between the literatures of the nineteenth and twentieth centuries. This was a bi-monthly review, founded by Professor Bogdan Popović. Even in the very beginning the *Glasnik* achieved high artistic and cultural standards, and it played the same role in Serbian literature that the *Revue des Deux-Mondes* played in nineteenth-century French literature. It gave young authors a way to reach a widening circle of readers.

Mirko Korolija, a Dalmatian poet whose first collected poems were published in 1914, has left a description of *Glasnik*'s role in the artistic life of the times. The offices of the newly-founded review were located at number 9 Skopljanska street in Belgrade, an address that was to become famous. Korolija wrote: "Skopljanska 9! Skopljanska 9! This thought, these two very simple words shine like two flashing buoys that sparkle and disappear . . . . For many years we sent our works to this address and waited for the final judgment, the word that would assign each writer his place . . . ."[4]

Along with the university and the *Glasnik*, the National Theater was an important cultural center. In its own way and for the times,

---

[4] Mirko Korolija, "Prvi put u začaranom krugu Jovana Skerlića," *Ideje*, godina I, broj 5, Beograd, 1934.

it was avant-garde. In Belgrade in 1911, it was quite bold to put Oscar Wilde's *Salome* in its repertory. The performance created quite a sensation. The theater was filled with a young and very enthusiastic audience. In their midst was Bojić, who did not miss one single performance. After the play, the offices of the *Srpski Književni Glasnik* were full of activity. The performance made a very strong impression, and the ensuing discussions were impassioned. The leading Serbian poet Jovan Dučić leaned on the editor's desk and read verses from *Salome*, while Bojić sat in silence and followed the whole scene with his fiery eyes. Skerlić, the strongest personality among those present, was making fun of everybody's enthusiasm. . . .[5]

A leading literary critic, Jovan Skerlić placed a high value on his "mission." He wanted to guide the youth of Serbia toward moral strength, national optimism, and logical reasoning. Though Skerlić admitted that in this world there might be moral suffering, weaknesses, and doubts, he demanded an active fight against them. He also demanded that there be a "real reason" for suffering. He loathed the vague pessimism and deep melancholy that were more and more often the leading themes of the new poetry. Skerlić considered them nothing but imitations of the morbid literatures of decadent Europe.[6] Every suffering had to be Cartesian and had to generate in man a reaction to fight. Suffering could only be converted into battle, and battle, according to him, had to lead to victory.

There are two possible reasons for Skerlić's views. The first was his temperament, which was that of a fighter, and, thus, more inclined to the optimism of victory than to the pessimism of defeat. The second was his deep-rooted conviction that the poet is responsible for the formation of ideals in new generations. He believed that literature must be strong and constructive itself in order to mold and guide strong and constructive youth.

It must be said that such an authoritarian concept could be imposed because of the particular times in which this generation found itself. Skerlić was writing when the Austro-Hungarian empire was carrying out the annexation of Bosnia and Herzegovina in 1908, and thus endangering the very existence of Serbia. In Skerlić's opinion, one of the first duties of literature was to save the culture and the spirit of the country. Thus, he strongly supported the writing of as

---

[5] *Ibid.*

[6] To fully comprehend Skerlić's hatred of "sick" emotions, it is necessary to point out his unfair judgment of the poetry of Vladislav Petković-Dis. For this, Skerlić himself coined a term: "Jedna književna zaraza" (A literary infection).

much patriotic poetry as possible. The young poets, among them Bojić, worked in an atmosphere of national optimism and enthusiasm, which came as a reaction to the serious dangers the country faced. They were deeply and earnestly involved in their poetry, which was for them more than the expression of their individual feelings. For them, poetry was no longer mere artistic pleasure: it was a vocation.

The new poets of the beginning of the century worked hard to create a new means of poetic expression able to communicate their answers to the vital problems of existence. Their creative output was slowed down by their efforts to polish their verses, but if the poems were fewer than in the nineteenth century, they were definitely superior.

The form of a poem became important for the aesthetic evaluation of poetry. This new concept was in contrast to the nineteenth-century idea that a poem was a spontaneous, unpolished expression of the original emotion. Thus, workmanship became another hallmark of the new poetry.

However, the evolution of form and the search for new poetic imagery were not the only elements that made the new poetry essentially different. The emotions at the very source of the poetic inspiration were becoming more and more sophisticated. The poet's inner life acquired a new sensitivity and seemed to embrace a much broader range. Nuances, unexplored in nineteenth-century Serbian poetry, became the basic concern of the young poets. The direct old-fashioned expressions such as "I love," "I desire," which had become the monotonous arsenal of the old poetry, yielded to the more nuanced "I dream," "I doubt."

The new poetry had not yet become abstract. Far from it—it was simply richer in shades and tried to evoke moods rather than to depict emotions. While Branko Radičević, Zmaj-Jovan Jovanić, and Vojislav Ilić, fitted their emotions into symmetrical verses, after the original tension had subsided, new poets tried to capture their moods while they were still alive. There was a noticeable change in the creative process itself; it was now simultaneous with the impact of the emotion. Thus, the new poetry gives the impression of being more mobile. Old poets attributed great importance to the shape and color of the eyes of the woman they loved; the new poets attempted to convey the mood that those eyes evoked in them. This in itself was a bold step forward.

A chronological survey of the poems published in the first decade of the twentieth century indicates that the previous summary is correct. The year 1901 saw the publication of *Pesme* (Poems) by Jovan Dučić, who with Rakić was destined to become the leading figure in modern Serbian poetry. This was the only major change for this year. However, it was also the year in which *Srpski Književni Glasnik* was founded. In the same year the collected poems of Dimitrije Gligorijević-Sokoljanin and Cvetko Janković appeared, but both poets brought nothing new to Serbian poetry and are now forgotten.

The year 1902 ushered in the first real change. *Srpski Književni Glasnik* had had time to become the first real herald of the new generation of poets. In this single year, *Glasnik* published poems without which no anthology of Serbian poetry could be imagined: Dučić: *Dubrovački Madrigal, Bdenje, Dubrovačko Veče*; Milan Rakić:[7] *Soneti, Hajka, Čekić bije o Čamovu dasku, Ljubavna Pesma, Dolap, Želja*: Milan Ćurčin; *Na Balu, Karnaval u Sumi, U Troje, Na Stranputici.*

By 1903, the collected poems of the new poets began to appear. Among the older poets, those still under the influence of the nineteenth century, Milorad Mitrović published *Pesme* (Poems), while the new poets were represented by the collected poems of Dučić, Rakić, and Stevan Luković. Their poems owed little to Vojislav Ilić, an influence that had for so long stifled the poets of the nineteenth century. These three collections of poems seemed to sum up the essential ideas and forms of the new poetry, the poetry that was to flourish in Serbia during the first two decades of the twentieth century.[8]

The following years were marked by publications of collected poems: in 1904, *Pesme* by Rakić and *Trenuci* by Danica Marković; in 1905, *Pesme* by Svetislav Stfanović. From then until the outbreak of the Balkan Wars, the period was filled with collections of poems by young poets, though many of these are now forgotten. Thus, the critic is understandably tempted to call the period from the founding of *Srpski Književni Glasnik* in 1901 to the outbreak of the Balkan Wars "The Golden Age of Serbian Poetry."

But Serbian poetry at the beginning of the twentieth century is not only a list of names and dates. Each poet has his own inspiration and versification, and each poem represents a different artistic personality. It would be difficult to recognize in the work of any of these poets the influences, foreign and domestic, that marked him most. At the time, influences were strong and varied. It is undoubtedly under the influence of Verlaine that Luković explored his inner moods in subtle and melodious analyses, even the most subtle moods

---

7 Milan Rakić published these poems in 1902 under the pseudonym *Z*.

8 In addition to these three collections of poems, Svetislav Stefanović published in Mostar, his original poems in 1903, with the addition of some translations, and Pijetro Kosorić published his *Pesme* in Užice. But these two collections are not as important as the ones previously mentioned.

of which he was barely aware. The symbolists, specifically Albert Samain, influenced Dučić and led him to spiritualize his emotions. There was, thus, in Dučić a synthesis of emotion and reason, an attempt to explain through spiritual symbols the slightest shades of his emotional life. The French "decadent" poets definitely influenced the extravagant and highly personal poetry of Milan Ćurčin, though in his particular case they reached him through the works of German secessionist poets. And Korolija is definitely under the influence of Gabriele D'Annunzio.

French artistic and literary ideas, once transplanted into a foreign milieu, were bound to change, a fact that sometimes makes it difficult to trace accurately some of the motifs in the new Serbian poetry;

During the last decade of the nineteenth century, *Vojislavism*[9] had prepared Serbian poetry for the acceptance of foreign influences. Vojislav Ilić cleared the ground for the coming influence, first of Parnassians and then Symbolists. At the same time, poetry became more important than prose in Serbian literature, since the new generation of writers consisted mostly of poets. This created a conflict between the clearly realistic tendencies in prose and individualistic idealism in poetry.

Two leading critics, Bogdan Popović and Jovan Skerlić, and two major poets, Milan Rakić and Jovan Dučić, helped spread French literary and aesthetic influences in Serbian poetry at the beginning of the century.

Bogdan Popović, professor of literature at the University of Belgrade, belonged to the French cultural orbit both intellectually and artistically and was deeply influenced by the aesthetic concepts of the Parnassian school. Hence his efforts to spread these concepts in the Serbian poetry of his time. Though he did not publish many critiques, *Srpski Književni Glasnik* and his own personal authority made him undoubtedly one of the leading critics of his time.

The second leading critic, Jovan Skerlić, was influenced by French literary aesthetics as well, but he soon found himself in complete opposition to any movement of *l'art pour l'art*. Skerlić used his influence to fight any egotistic or decadent movement energetically. His concepts on literary aesthetics were so strongly influenced by his nationalistic ideology that he often reacted to artistic problems more as a national and political thinker than as an art critic. For example,

---

[9] *Vojislavism*, a movement in Serbian poetry, was derived from and named after the poet Vojislav Ilić. This style was particularly influential during the last decade of the nineteenth century.

he strongly praised Maurice Magre, not for the beauty of his verses, but for his moral health and intense vitality. Skerlić demanded that health and vitality be the basic elements of Serbian modern poetry and for these reasons, the wrong ones, praised Bojić's early poems, which deserved praise of a different sort.

Skerlić wished the new Serbian poetry to be clear, intense, and straightforward. His article "*Jedna Književna Zaraza*" ("A Literary Infection"), shows how repulsed he was by what he termed, with utter contempt, "decadence." Above all, he feared the influence of foreign, decadent poetry on the new Serbian poetry, since he never lost sight of his concept that poetry should serve to build a healthy and strong new generation. Thus, he fought against the pessimistic and somber tones in the new poems, and he detested the foreign poetic movements of *cainism, satanism*, and, generally speaking, all the modern *isms*. Every time his basic concept was challenged, Skerlić ruthlessly defended it.

The two great Serbian poets of the early twentieth century were Milan Rakić and Jovan Dučić. Rakić was in full agreement with the aesthetic ideals of the Parnassians, while Dučić was strongly influenced by the Symbolists. The impact of these Parnassian and Symbolist influences is easily recognized, either directly in the poems of Rakić and Dučić, or indirectly in the works of the poets they themselves influenced. This gave way to two distinct foreign influences, mostly French: one taken at its source, and one transmitted through the works of the two great native poets.

However, the succession of poetic movements in Serbia and France do not match chronologically. In the second half of the nineteenth century, about 1860, while the Parnassians were taking over the Romantics in France, Romanticism was barely reaching its peak in Serbia. This Romanticism most often took the form of patriotic poems, and an exalted enthusiasm. Thus, Serbia lived through a period of national romanticism between 1860 and 1870. The Congress of Berlin, which gave Bosnia and Herzegovina to Austro-Hungary, cut short that enthusiasm and the dreams of the Serbian romantic movement as well.

The moment had come for Vojislav Ilić to introduce "modern realism," a movement that strongly influenced poets at the turn of the century, into Serbian poetry. But Ilić did not create a poetic school in the full sense of the word. His influence was extraordinarily powerful, but gave birth to no well-defined program or established aesthetic dogmas. It was spontaneous and achieved through Ilić's numerous poems. By introducing the young poets to a better appreciation of foreign literatures and by preparing the ground for the critics Bogdan Popović and Jovan Skerlić, it contributed to the formation of a modern poetry.

Ilić opposed the melodious romanticism of the nineteenth century and all its exaltations; instead, he created a poetry of calm and disciplined emotions *(poezija mirnog čuvstva)*. In this way, he paved the way for the influence of the Parnassians. One of his essential characteristics was his sense of plastic beauty, so attuned to the Parnassian concept of sculptural imagery. Instead of relying on melodious sound effects, Ilić's imagery is visual. Thus, between 1885 and 1900, Vojislav Ilić prepared the way for the French Parnasse and indicated the direction in which twentieth-century Serbian poetry was to develop.

The highest achievements of this new poetry are doubtlessly the poems of Milan Rakić and Jovan Dučić. Though their artistic concepts and the form of their poems differ greatly, these two poets are without equals in Serbian modern poetry.

In the twentieth century the new poets were influenced both by Rakić and Dučić and by their appreciation and love of foreign literatures, which had grown stronger and stronger from the times of Vojislav Ilić to those of Bogdan Popović, Skerlić, Rakić, and Dučić. These two sources are easily discernible in the new poetry of the twentieth century, with all its intricate currents and movements.

At the basis of any exchange of influences there must be a harmony of sensitivities. The early poetry of Milutin Bojić shows the influence of Baudelaire's exalted sensuality. That influence is quite different from Baudelaire's influence on Pandurović and Dis, both of whom were fascinated primarily by the French poet's morbid emotions and his predilection for cemeteries. None of these morbid motifs can be found in Bojić's poetry, just as no exalted sensuality can be found in Pandurović or Dis.

Nevertheless, all the young poets had one thing in common; they all stood for a complete break with the old school of the nineteenth century, each of them in his own personal way.

The versification and poetic language of the nineteenth century seemed to be cast in an iron mold, just as French poetry was at the outbreak of Romanticism. Some words, according to very precise rules of usage, had full poetic citizenship, while others were outlawed and exiled to other linguistic regions. In the Serbian poetic language of the nineteenth century, expressions such as "slender waist" and "pale brow" were dedicated to emotions of unhappy love. Ilić imposed his poetic imagery of "fatal ruins," "cold marble," and "unfaithful sweethearts" *(Kobne ruševine, hladan mermer, neverne drage)*

Thus, the new poetry was in search of a new verse, more fluid and better able to suggest broader, deeper, less visual images. At its start, it hesitated between the verses of eight, fourteen, or even sixteen syllables, the latter a heritage from Ilić's versification. But one concept emerged clearly. The new verse had to be precise in rhythm, and it had to be symmetrical.

Rakić and Dučić gave the leading role in the new Serbian versification to eleven- and twelve-syllable verses, which became essential in the new poetry at the beginning of the twentieth century. "Since the beginning of the twentieth century no one has gone farther in the polishing of verse than we did," declared Milan Rakić.[10] These eleven- and twelve-syllable verses became the only ones capable of expressing the new artistic aspirations. They were doubtlessly imposed by Rakić and Dučić, because their brilliant poems seemed, even from the first day they appeared, to have created a firm pattern. Rakić and Dučić were thus responsible for restricting the new poetry to their own versifications. It became exceedingly difficult for new poets to free themselves from the almost perfect form that Rakić and Dučić had achieved immediately.

Though the eleven- and twelve-syllable verses seemed to be the only form capable of expressing the new poetic ideals, the fact remains that these verses could always be treated in new and original rhythmical patterns. Thus, though Bojić mostly used twelve-syllable verse, his versification is not in the least reminiscent of either Rakić or Dučić. It is definitely his own. It was always possible for the new poets to cut the rhythm of a twelve-syllable verse in an infinite number of ways.

All the apparent differences in the works of the young new poets make it difficult to systematize the artistic achievements of these years or to classify them into definite schools. Rakić and Dučić remain the spearhead of what seems to be a disparate troupe of creative artists. Their followers are individuals, with different tendencies, emotions, moods, aesthetic concepts, and, most important, varying degrees of talent. The differences are too great to allow anyone to fit them into rigid patterns.

The literary critic Skerlić died too young, too early in a promising career to have had the time to give a more systematic judgment of the period in his *Istorija Srpske Književnosti* (History of Serbian Literature). Many young poets, like Bojić, had not yet published enough poems at Skerlić's death to enable him to evaluate their work, though it must be recognized that the prognoses Skerlić made were generally accurate and that the young poets he praised lived up to his expectations.

---

[10] Milan Rakić, as quoted by Branimir Ćosić, *Deset Pisaca, Deset Razgovora*, Belgrade, 1935.

Among the new poets, Stevan Luković reaches a tonality of sincere melancholy. His poems are in a minor key, and his verse has a great fluidity. His dreamlike quality, his use of symbols, and his essentially elegaic melodies classify him as a basically lyric poet, in the vein of Verlaine and Dante Gabriel Rossetti. Ćurčin, on the other hand, is bizarre, highly original, and one of the first poets to introduce free verse into Serbian poetry. His bold irony is expressed in novel and original verses. Thus, Ćurčin often is a necessary antidote to the sophistication and elegance of Dučić. Proka Jovkić echoes the clarion of battle trumpets that introudce the motif of non-compromising ideals, and his strength and vitality thus clash sharply with the pessimism of Vladislav Petković-Dis. The poetry of Pandurović is in the same vein as Dis's pessimism. But Pandurović contributed high melodic quality and explored the depths of his heart, thus introducing a nuanced emotional analysis into the new Serbian poetry. Velimir Rajić, after having lived through deep personal sufferings, left an intimate poetry of neither social nor philosophical concern. But the trans-position of his personal sufferings into purely lyric verses had a great nobility of tone and thus reached a high ethical level. Rajić remains one of the great lyric poets of his time, although Skerlić deprived him of the place he rightfully deserves, unable as the critic was to condone the deep personal pessimism of Rajić. In contrast to Rajić, Šantić contributed emotional warmth and the depth of genuine patriotism.

It is difficult to classify so many successful poets, primarily because of the important differences in tehir artistic concepts. Literary critics more or less agree on their respective worth, but they cannot agree on a classification into schools and movements.

The outbreak of the Balkan Wars, first the Serbo-Turk War of 1912, and then the Serbo-Bulgar War of 1913, brought about a fundamental change in the literary scene. Though both wars were short, they took their toll in human lives, including several young and promising talents. Both wars also created an even deeper awareness of the impending national danger, which resulted in a great increase in the number of patriotic poems. Young poets who had published mostly love poems now turned toward patriotic poetry. Among those was Milutin Bojić.

But the real change was to come with the outbreak of World War I, and, in the case of Serbia, with 1915. On October 26, 1915, the last inch of Serbian soil was lost to the enemy; the Albanian exodus began, as did the sufferings of the women and children who remained in the occupied territory. The horrors the occupying forces perpetrated on the civil population in Serbia during World War I as well as the sacrifice of the army and refugees during the Albanian exodus are both well-known. It is difficult to describe, in fiction or non-fiction, the martyrdom of a nation that refused to disown its identity during those tragic and agonizing days.

Milutin Bojić lived through agony day by day. He survived the Albanian exodus, the hopelessness of Corfu, and finally succumbed to tuberculosis in Thessaloniki. From all this came his *Pesme Bola i Ponosa* (Poems of Suffering and Pride), which are admirable works of art and faith as well.

The survivors of the exodus had an incredible dedication and vitality—dedication to a great cause and the vitality of victorious sacrifice. The suffering of the people and their faith in the future are the two main motifs of Serbian poetry during World War I. These were not only the two essential literary themes, but also the two basic concepts of the Serbian people at the time.

Because of their faith in the future, Serbs relinquished neither their freedom nor their culture. The oldest newspaper, *Novine Srpske*, moved from Belgrade to Niš in 1915 and stopped publishing only during the exodus. At Corfu, in 1916, the paper resumed publication. It had the privilege to gather around it, along with its duty to publish official announcements and news from the front, what was left of the literary community. Thus, *Novine Srpske* expressed in poetry and prose the life and ideals of a whole nation.

As early as April 2, 1917, *Novine Srpske* published a supplement *Zabavnik*, which showed a concern for the survival of Serbian literature and art. The purpose of *Zabavnik* was twofold. On one hand, it affirmed the survival of Serbian literature; on the other, it proved how Serbia would inevitably survive the war. From this second theme, which was not simply the belief of a small group of people but the faith of a whole nation, came most literary themes. Poets dedicated their poems either to the tragedy of their nation or to the glory of the national past. They sensed that the historic past was deeply linked to the tragic present. The moral ideal on which all this literature is based is best expressed in this verse by Milosav Jelić: "Srčan vitez duše milostivne" ("A brave knight with a merciful soul").

Love poems are exceedingly rare during this period. This clearly shows how tragically the combat had affected the entire nation. With time, love poems were bound to reappear. But even then, amazingly enough, they do not come from the pen of young poets, but rather from the older poets, for whom this was an established genre.

All Serbian poetry of these years revealed deep concepts of suffering and combat, or as Milutin Bojić entitled his last collection of poems: *Poems of Suffering and Pride*.

But *Novine Srpske* was not the only paper in which Serbian literature survived. Also published were: *La Patrie Serbe* (in French), *Le Bulletin Yougoslave* (also in French), *Srpski Glasnik, Velika Srbija, Napred* (with an edition translated into French under the title *En Avant*), and *Jovan Skerlić*, a paper published by Serbian students who had survived the exodus and were living in France, where they created an entire literature, which for want of means, was hand-copied. They circulated hand-copied books, such as Njegoš' *Gorski Vijenac* (The Mountain Wreath), Mažuranić's *Smrt Smail-Age Čengića* (The Death of Smail-Aga Čengić), and a whole anthology of Serbian poetry. This little-known effort is worthy of great respect..

During the exile, Serbian poets published their works in newspapers. Very few collections of poems were published separately; nevertheless, there were several noteworthy collections: Miloslav Jelić's *Srbijanski Venac* (The Serbian Wreath); Dragutin Filipović's *Kosovski Božuri* (The Peonies of Kosovo); and Milutin Bojić's *Pesme Bola i Ponosa* (Poems of Suffering and Pride). Those who published their works in newspapers are: Dučić, Dis, Bojić, Vladimir Stanimirović, Dragutin Filipović, Stevan Bešević, Stanislav Vinaver, Božidar Kulić, and many others less well-known. Among prose authors were Ivo Ćipiko, Nikola Daničić, and Zarije Popović-Devečerski. In literary criticism, Pavle Popović published reviews and articles in order to inform foreign readers of the problems and achievments of Serbian literature.[11]

---

[11] Serbian literature was not the only one to concentrate on the war. Similar themes became a widespread phenomenon in Western literature. In French literature, Anatole France published *Ce que disent les morts*, and *Sur la voie* de la gloire; Maurice Barrès, who was already famous for his novels of *"énergie nationale"*, wrote *L'Amitié dans les tranchées* and *La croix de guerre*. Henri Bergson was meditating on the meaning of war, while Paul Fort published his *Les poésies de la France*. Paul Adam, René Bazin, Rémy de Gourmont and Charles Péguy died on the battlefield. English literature followed the same pattern, as did the Belgian, Italian, and tohers. Rudyard Kipling wrote poems for his son, who was killed in the war, and also wrote *France at War* and *The Eyes of Asia*. H. G. Wells published *The War That Will Kill the War*, and other novels. D'Annunzio, who was not yet the staunch supporter of Italian expansion in Dalmatia, praised Serbia and Belgium. Emile Verhaeren gave the beautiful *La Belgique sanglante* and *Parmi les ruines*, while Maeterlinck wrote *Les ruines de la guerre* and *L'Hôte inconnu*.

Of special interest is a whole branch of literature dedicated to Serbia by foreign writers. Innumerable memoirs were written to prove: "I, too, was there when an unbelievable tragedy occurred." Many poems were dedicated to Serbia, and among them, undoubtedly the most beautiful is *Les quatre boeufs du roi Pierre*, by Edmond Rostand.

Serbian literature, as well as the Serbian nation, was bled almost to death by World War I. This is not a figure of speech, but a cruel fact. According to the obituaries and requiems published by *Novine Srpske* in Greece, the following Serbian poets and writers died during the war: Nikola Antula, in Macedonia, 1917; Jovan Varagić, poet, killed as a hostage in Bosnia, 1915; Miloš Vidaković, poet, Macedonia, 1915; Vlado Gaćinović, poet, 1917; Nikola Daničić, prose writer, typhoid, 1917; Jovan Živanović, a student and poet, burned alive in Višegrad, 1914; Proka Jovkić, poet, typhoid, 1915; Milan Luković, poet, 1914; Vladislav Petković-Dis, poet, died aboard a torpoed ship, 1917; Uroš Petrović, University professor, died in Albania, 1915; Velimir Rajić, poet, typhoid, 1915; Milutin Bojić, poet, tuberculosis, 1917; Milutin Uskoković, novelist, committed suicide on leaving the country, 1915; Slavko Krčevinac, editor of *The Republic*, killed 1914; Dr. Djordje Lazarević, died as a hostage in Bosnia, 1915; Petar Petrović-Ćela, killed 1914; Risto Radulović, died in an Austrian camp, 1915; Vladislav Ribnikar, 1915; Darko Ribnikar, 1914; Dimitrije Jocović, 1914; and many, many others, less well-known, but who, nonetheless, were promising young writers.

The end of World War I, the return of the Serbian army to the liberated country, and the political, social, and moral changes that occurred in the ensuing period created new approaches and new achievements in art and literature. The poetry of Milutin Bojić, which had been destroyed by fire during the war in Niš and Thessaloniki, was published now under unfavorable conditions, since it spoke about sacrifice and tragedy to an audience that wanted to live and, if possible, to forget. Only twenty years later, on the eve of World War II, did new generations rediscover Milutin Bojić. Since then the appreciation of his poetic work as well as his personal fame as a poet have grown steadily. Today he is considered one of the best poets in twentieth-century Serbian literature.

MILUTIN BOJIĆ, BIOGRAPHY

Milutin Bojić was born in Belgrade on May 7, 1892. At the time his parents lived at No. 4 Sremska Street, in an old-fashioned house destined to be destroyed in the bombardment of 1944. The family was originally from Herzegovina. His father was a self-employed shoemaker, whose ornate slippers were much sought after by the ladies of Belgrade. His earnings were sufficient to ensure a comfortable living for the whole family.

Jovan and Sofija Bojić had five children; three sons, and two daughters. The sons were Milutin, Radivoje, and Dragoljub, the daughters Jelica and Danica.[1] The couple lived modestly in a small apartment located just above the shop and thus were able to save the money to buy a new home on Hilendarska Street in 1902.[2]

The poet's mother, Sofija, was a relative of the well-known writer Stevan Sremac. The family, however, kept closer ties with his brother, Jovan Sremac, a plumber by trade, who had moved from Vranje to Belgrade before Milutin was born. Members of the family said that Jovan greatly influenced the young poet by introducing him to Serbian folk tales and legends.

In 1905, when Milutin was thirteen years old, the family moved into the house in Hilendarska Street, an old house with a beautiful garden. By acquiring it, Jovan Bojić fulfilled a dream cherished by all small artisans in Belgrade: to own a house where he could retire with security in his old age. However, this was not to be his fate; Jovan Bojić died in 1911 at the age of fifty-six, only six years after moving into his new home. Thus, at the age of nineteen, Milutin became head of the family and thereby responsible for his mother, younger brothers and sisters. Until his death, during all the tragic years of war and exile, he was to remain faithful to this great responsibility.

Milutin spent his adolescence and the Balkan Wars of 1912 to 1914 in this house. He had his own room, in which he wrote his first poems and dramas in verse.

---

[1] Radivoje Bojić made a diplomatic career in the Ministry of Foreign Affairs. He was also a writer and published *Ujakov Vinograd* in 1923, and *Zmije na Asfaltu* in 1933. Dragoljub Bojić taught geography in Belgrade High School. Jelica Bojić-Nikolić married and lived in Belgrade. Danica Bojić died single in Belgrade.

[2] At the turn of the century, conditions in Belgrade were favorable for artisans to develop small enterprises of their own.

There is evidence that Milutin began writing poetry at a very early age. Dravić writes:

> One of my pupils has been writing poetry since the first years of elementary school. His father, a shoemaker on Sremska Street, is very proud of his son's work. He keeps the poems locked in his safe as great treasures, convinced that they are of immense value and proof of his son's brilliant future.[3]

Milutin Bojić left elementary school in 1902, and in the fall of the same year enrolled in the "Realka" High School. Fortunately, his high school and university records were not destroyed in the ensuing wars, and we have proof today that he was an excellent student. Because of his superior scholastic record he was exempt from the final oral examinations.[4] During the summer of 1908, while still in high school, Bojić wrote his first drama in verse, *Slepi Despot* (The Blind Despot).[5] which he intended to read at the meeting of the High School Literary Organization. The title page bears the inscription in the poet's own handwriting that this is only the first part of a dramatic trilogy to be entitled *Despotova Kruna* (The Crown of the Despot).

In the following year, the poet came under the influence of Milutin K. Dragutinović, his high school teacher of Serbian Language and Literature, a writer of theatrical reviews for *Delo*, and at the same time a member of the artistic committee of the Belgrade National Theater. In 1911, it was to him that Bojić submitted his drama *Lanci*, as his entry in that year's competition. Through the influence of Dragutinović, Bojić became a dedicated participant in high school literary activities and by the end of his high school studies became Chairman of the school's Literary Club. One of his friends, Radoslav Vesnić, has left a written record of that period.

> When he wrote *Slepi Despot*, Bojić was still a high school student, president or vice-president of the school's Literary Club. The drama was written after the annexation of Bosnia and Herzegovina, in the autumn of 1908. I immediately took the

---

[3] Jovan Dravić, "Uspomene na Bojića," (*Delo*, Knjiga 60, June 1912). This article is reliable, since it was published in 1912, before Bojić became famous. Dravić was in charge of teaching Serbian language and literature in the elementary school Bojić attended. Dravić later contacted Jeremija Zivanović, editor of *Venac*, and showed him Bojić's poems *Vrane* and *Prvi Čovek* (The Crows, and The First Man).

[4] High school grades were on a scale ranging from 1 to 5, and Milutin's were all 5's His studies were particularly good in 1907, and at the end of that academic year he was publicly recognized as the best student of the year.

[5] The manuscript of *Slepi Despot* is presently in the National Library in Belgrade.

> manuscript and read it. The next day I went to see Mr. Rista Odavić, then the dramatic director of the National Theater. Odavić accepted the manuscript with a smile and told me to come and see him a few days later. His reception was very friendly . . . .[6]

Odavić liked the young Bojic's drama in verse. As soon as Vesnić learned of Odavić's favorable opinion, he went to see Bojić. Vesnić writes:

> I found him in his room. I took him by the hand and drew him out of the room. We ran together. When Odavić saw Bojić's large, black eyes, he exclaimed 'These are eyes of a poet! These eyes can never betray! You are the poet of *Slepi Despot*![7]

After graduation from high school, Bojić had to decide on the course of his further studies. Though his father was very proud of Milutin's poetic achievements, he wanted his son to gain financial security in a more practical field. But Milutin was drawn to literature and, as a result of his confidence in his own talent and the dedication he felt for the literary vocation, Milutin Bojić enrolled at the School of Philosophy at the University of Belgrade in the autumn of 1910.

At the university Bojić regularly attended Branislav Petronijević's courses in philosophy. These were survey courses and covered, for the academic year 1910-1911: "The History of Modern Philosophy from Descartes to Kant;" and for 1911-1912: "The History of Modern Philosophy from Kant until Today." According to Professor Miodrag Ibrovac, Bojić was one of the best students Petronijević had in that generation. Ibrovac also recalls in an oral interview that Bojić's work in literature under the eminent professors Bogdan and Pavle Popović was not so successful. In any case, Professor Bogdan Popović taught "The History of Italian Literature" in 1910-1911; and "The History of German Literature" in 1911-1912. Professor Pavle Popović taught "The History of Southern Slavic Literatures" in 1910-1911, and "The History of Literature in Dubrovnik" in 1911-1912.

While still in the university Bojić began his collaboration with *Pijemont*, a daily paper published from 1911 to 1915, with only a short interruption in the fall of 1912, when its owner and editor-in-chief, Ljuba Jovanović-Čupa, was at the front fighting in the Serbo-Turk war. The paper was the quasi-official voice of the league of officers, who, under the name *Ujedinjenje ili Smrt* (Black Hand),

---

6 Radoslav Vesnić, "Slepi Despot, Neobjavljena i izgubljena drama *M. Bojića,*" *Venac*, Knjiga XV, 1929.

7 *Ibid.*

played an important role in the political life of the time. As the voice of the ultra-nationalist right wing, *Pijemont* opposed the radical policies of Nikola Pašić, repeatedly attacking his lack of action and firmness in dealing with national problems.[8] During his journalistic career with the *Pijemont*, however, Bojić never published any political articles or commentaries. He contributed only theatrical reviews.

The considerable amount of work that Bojić produced during these years as a student, journalist, and poet, did not prevent him from enjoying life. He worked during the day, but he reserved evenings and nights for the enjoyment of life and its pleasures. He was fond of fashionable clothes, even rather extravagant ones, and was, for example, one of the first young men in Belgrade to wear a tuxedo. This was considered extremely bold at the time.

During these years, the wealthy merchants of Belgrade began to invite artists and promising writers into their homes. Prominent political and economic leaders more and more acted as art patrons, though still on a limited scale. Ljuba Jovanović-Patak and his wife Simka greatly helped Bojić in this respect, particularly during the war and the retreat of the Serbian army through Albania, as well as during his stay and illness in Greece. Marko Trifković and his wife Mara supported writers from Bosnia and Herzegovina, including Sibe Miličić. Editors of literary magazines helped young writers and gave them a chance to publish their works. One example was Dragoljub Pavlović, editor-in-chief of *Delo*, to whom Bojić owed the publication of his first poems.

Milutin Bojić was an impulsive young man. From rare photographs and the testimony of his contemporaries emerges the figure of a young man of medium stature, with slightly stooped shoulders, thick brown hair, and a pale oval face. His eyebrows were dark, and one of them was almost always raised, giving his face an expression of intense irony. His eyes burned with constant passion, and his lips were full and sensuous. There was also something young and vulnerable in his smile. He smiled often, and his conversation was reputed to be brilliant.

According to his contemporaries, he was extemely proud, and therefore very vulnerable. Undoubtedly, these reports were exaggerated after he became famous; when he was eighteen, he was probably no more proud and vulnerable than any young man with an intense

---

8 The first owner and editor-in-chief of *Pijemont* was Ljuba Jovanović-Čupa, who died of typhoid fever in the war of 1913. He was succeeded as editor-in-chief by Branislav Božović, but the 1915 Albanian Exodus put an end to *Pijemont*.

inner life. The Czechoslovakian writer, Helena Marližova, describes him as "smiling and brilliant." Miss Marližova met Bojic during 1913, while she was a volunteer nurse with the 17th Reserve Hospital of the 7th Regiment.

> His spirit was in constant opposition to everything, and at the same time he was an enthusiast. He was bursting with desires, and he drank the sap of life through his senses. He made fun of my pronunciation of the soft 'lj' without mercy and no respect at all for the author in me. I felt he was very close to me in his sense of caricature, which he turned against himself as well.[9]

---

[9] This is from a conversation between Helena Marližova and Jovan Kršić in Prague, quoted by Jovan Kršić in his article "Nepoznata Pesma Bojićeva, Zelene Oči," *Srpski Književni Glasnik*, Knjiga XXX, Nova Serija, 1930. Miss Marližova was then the wife of the writer Ivan Olbracht and had published translations of two poems by Bojić in the literary magazine *Svetozar* in 1913. The poems she translated are: *Smrt Majke Jurovića* and *Zelene Oči*, both written for her by Bojić.

At times the young man's pride and the violent reactions caused him to lose sight of proportions. When his ego had been hurt, objective values seemed not to exist. In 1911, a contest was organized by the Literary Committee of the National Theater in Belgrade to select the best play of the year. Forty-two new plays were entered, including *Gospodja sa suncobranom* (The Lady with the Umbrella), by Ivo Vojnović, an adaptation of *Narodni Poslanik* (The People's Representative), by Nušić, *Hasanaginica* (Hassan-Aga's Wife), by Šantić, *Zulumćár* (Zulumćár—A Local Turkish Terrorist), and *Povratak* (The Return), by Ćorović, and *Paraputa* (Paraputa—Personal Nickname), by Borisav Stanković, all works by well-known and experienced writers. *Lanci* (The Chains), a drama presented by Bojić, was among the works not rejected after the first reading. Unfortunately, the drama was lost during World War I, and so we must trust the opinion of Jeremija Živanović, then a member of the Committee. According to Živanović, it was immediately evident that the author was a very young man who believed he had uncovered the truth and had presented it in life's most intricate problems. The drama's hero seems to have reflected Bojić's youthful exaggerations and naive concepts. The jury was unable to consider it for the final award.

Bojić was extremely popular among the young writers and poets of his generation, as well as in the Bohemian and artistic circles of Belgrade's night life. He seems to have had an extraordinary vitality and a vivid sense of humor. Miss Radmila Todorović[10] showed me a scrap of paper found in Bojic's room in Thessaloniki, the very same room from which he was taken to the hospital to die. On this scrap of paper Bojić had written: "My pleasures: 1.— women, 2.— a beautiful landscape, 3.—books, museums, theater, 4.— cigarettes, 5.—wine."

Though he loved life and all its pleasures, Bojić worked hard, both at his art and his studies. Thus, the years between 1910 and 1914 were for him a period of great artistic achievement. He filled them with hard work, laughter, and sunshine.

At the outbreak of World War I, Bojić had almost finished his studies at the University of Belgrade. Through the first months of war and until the spring of 1915, he remained employed at *Pijemont*.

---

translations of two poems by Bojic in the literary magazine *Svetozar* in 1913. The poems she translated are: *Smrt Majke Jogovica* and *Zelene Oci*, both written for her by Bojic.

[10] Radmila Todorović, daughter of Col. Todorović and Mrs. Todorović, née Dragičević, was Bojić's fiancée. She was born in 1895 and died in Belgrade in 1971. She never married after his death. I am indebted to her for unpublished letters, notes, poems, photographs, as well as for oral information about Bojić.

At the beginning of the exodus of 1915, he moved his entire family, for which he was responsible, to Niš. He did not think he was leaving his home town and carefree youth forever. But a whole nation was beginning its retreat and entering the long and tragic road that was to lead the poet to exile and death.

Bojić had assumed the responsibility for his mother, two brothers, and two sisters, and in Niš, besides his regular army position as censor of the military mail, he published articles in *Niški Glasnik* to meet his financial obligations to his numerous family. However, he devoted his real efforts during this period to an epic poem he was writing in his few moments of free time. Bojić finished the poem, *Cain*, while still in Niš and published it just prior to the final exodus of the army. The entire poem is patriotic and is based on a comparison between Bulgaria's attack on Serbia and Cain's murder of Abel. When they occupied Niš, the Bulgarians burned the entire edition, and the only copy that survived was the one Bojić carried through Albania in his knapsack. This copy was to serve as the basis for the second edition which was printed after the war.

In 1915, Milutin's mother, Sofija Bojić, died in Niš of cancer. As the enemy was then invading Serbia, Bojić had to flee the country with his brother Radivoje, leaving behind his brother Dragoljub, who was too young to follow the retreat, and his two sisters.

The enemy occupation of the country cut the family in two. Milutin and Radivoje Bojić retreated with the army, while Dragoljub and the two sisters remained in occupied Serbia. The first leg of the two brothers' journey took them through Kraljevo, to Kruševac, Kuršumlija, and finally to Mitrovica. After a stop in Mitrovica, they continued to Priština, Prizren, Djakovica, Dečane, and Péc. From Péc they began the tragic crossing of the Albanian mountains—through Čakor, Andrijevica, and Montenegro—and the descent to Scutari via Podgorica.[11]

During these tragic days it was often difficult simply to be human, and even more difficult to be kind and charitable. But Bojić managed to be both. A companion who shared the exodus with him recalls:

> From the very first days he shared the bread he was carrying in his knapsack. I asked him what was he going to do in the days ahead. He simply answered 'Don't even ask! There will be some coffee and sugar left![12]

---

11 The poet Milan Ćurčin went with Bojić as far as Scutari, and Vojislav Jovanović-Marambo was with him for the second part. I am indebted to these two literary men for retracing the route of Bojić's exodus.

12 Stojan Živadinović, *Venac*, Knjiga IX, 1929.

During the snowstorms and exhausting marches through the mountains, Bojić began writing his *Pesme Bola i Ponosa* (Poems of Suffering and Pride), in which he undertook to record the pride and grandeur that underlay the sacrifice of a whole people. One evening, in the snows of the barren Montenegrin mountains, he told his friend Stojan Živadinović,

> You do not realize what you are missing by sleeping. In circumstances like these, the entire soul must be kept constantly awake. Centuries have never painted such a vast fresco. Never was death so greedy, nor were heroes so indifferent to it.[13]

While starving men fell half-dead to the frozen ground for a few hours of rest, Bojić sat awake for whole nights, feeling within the depths of his soul the grandeur of the almost dream-like tragedy. Those who knew him during this exodus unanimously declared that he suffered far more from the tragedy of his country and his people than from his own pain. The poems of suffering and pride he composed during those days are evidence of this.

Stojan Živadinović, in the article previously cited, gives a description of Bojić during these days:

> He was dressed in a strange way. A *šajkača* (a kind of cloth-made hat without a brim) was pulled to the front of his head and almost completely covered his forehead. His eyebrows were hardly visible. Under its weight, the ears seemed to collapse. He wore a kind of long, black coat, covered with mud and held in place by a string. He used another piece of string for a belt, and from it hung a pot for boiling water, a tea strainer, a canteen, and many other useful things. He walked, slightly bent forward, followed everywhere by the noise of the things clashing at his waist.[14]

In his cloth-bag he carried the only surviving copy of his epic poem *Kain* as well as the first pages of a new drama in verse he had begun, *Uroševa Ženidba* (The Marriage of Uroš). The *Pesme Boli i Ponosa* (Poems of Pride and Suffering) slowly matured in him. He also dreamed of transposing the imagery of medieval Byzantium into Serbian verse, and thus of giving new directions to Serbian poetry after the war. Stanislav Vinaver, a Serbian poet and literary critic, writes that he and Bojić

> spent three entire hours talking about Byzantium and the possibility of transposing it into Serbian art. We also spoke about the style that future Serbian poetry should assume. Bojić foresaw the reign of epic genre as the only possible form that could do justice to recent historical events. Personally, I believed in the coming of a period of mysticism.[15]

---

13 *Ibid.*

14 *Ibid.*

15 Stanislav Vinaver, "Skerlić and Bojić," *Pravda*, newspaper, January 6, 9, and 10, 1935, as well as April 20, 1935, Belgrade.

On the other hand, Stojan Živadinović writes,

> I shall never forget the day when we saw the sea. Only then did Bojić begin to speak about the future. He was making plans for a vast novel in verse, for comedies, dramas, tragedies, all intended to bring the great events of our history back to life.[16]

From Scutari, Bojić continued the exodus to San Giovanni. From there, he hoped to sail to France aboard the ship that took Field Marshal Putnik, other ailing officers, and a number of civilian refugees. But since he was a soldier, he had to stay, and the ship took his fiancee Miss Todorović and his young brother Radivoje to France without him.

Even during these days, Bojić continued to read. Among Miss Todorović's papers are unpublished letters that Bojić wrote to her and to his brother Radivoje in France, letters in which he speaks of his literary interests. In a letter from Corfu to his brother Radivoje on September 19, 1916, Bojić wrote:

> I have left Chateaubriand for the time being. I read Vigny and the Memoirs by Saint-Simon. Waiting for me are the complete works of Corneille. I shall send you my translation of a poem by Rostand, which will be of interest to the French.[17]

In another letter, also to Radivoje, on October 30, 1916, he wrote:

> I am spending my days here reading. Soon I shall have finished the complete works of Chateaubriand. I am also reading Vigny's novels and Saint-Simon's frightening *Memoirs* on the court of Louis XIV, doubtlessly the best book of this genre. I am also reading Corneille's works. . . .[18]

All the while, Bojić was also writing. At the end of 1915, while still in Scutari, he began his collection of sonnets and at the same time published separately in *Srpske Novine* the poems that were to be collected in 1917 under the title *Pesme Bola i Ponosa* (Poems of Suffering and Pride). In the same paper, *Srpske Novine*, he published parts of an epic poem, *Večna Straza* (The Eternal Sentinel), a poem that he never completed. He was also finsishing his drama in verse, *Uroševa Ženidba* (The Marriage of Uros).

Pesme Bola i Ponosa were released in Thessaloniki in 1917, shortly before the poet's death. The original edition was completely destroyed by the great fire of Thessaloniki, and the only copy that survived was the one the poet sent to his fiancée, Miss Todorović, in France.

---

16 Stojan Živadinović, *Venac*, Knjiga IX, 1929.

17 Segments of Bojić's unpublished letters are the property of Miss Radmila Todorović and are printed here with her permission.

18. *Ibid*.

This copy is the basis of the post-war edition. In barely two years, two of Bojic's published works were destroyed by fire, one intentionally by the enemy and the other by accident. At a time when these poems, especially the *Pesme Bola i Ponosa* (Poems of Suffering and Pride), would have meant so much to an entire nation, they were not available, and when they were published after the war, the emotional climate had changed.

In August, 1916, Bojić received a month's leave and sailed for France. He spent this month in Nice with Miss Todorović.

According to his nephew, Dragoslav Nikolić, Bojić caught cold one evening in September of 1917, while sitting with friends on the terrace of a cafe in Thessaloniki. His friends advised him to put on an overcoat, for the weather had turned abruptly chilly, but the poet only laughed and refused. The cold developed into pneumonia, which in turn progressed rapidly into tuberculosis.

Owing to the influence of Ljuba Jovanović-Patak, the poet was admitted to the army hospital Prestolonaslednikova Bolnica, where Jovanović's wife frequently visited him. But the illness developed rapidly, and the poet was very soon lost.

While in the hospital, the poet composed poems of melancholy and hopelessness for the first time. Miss Todorović showed me a poem found in the poet's papers after his death. It is written on a scrap of paper, which bears the stamp of the hospital:

Like a dead body without will or strength
I neither hear, nor see, nor feel any more.
Black raindrops are singing above my head
The deep pain born from happy memories.

Boredom with her retinue of sadness
Tortures me and burns like poison.
Dead are my faith and self-assurance,
My brow is creased and furrowed by worries.

Everything in me cries and laments;
I am mortified for there is no more
Strength left in my heart, only death
Where once were melodies of happy days

I don't even know how to laugh any more,
My own words are painful and consume me.
Oh, my spring, death is, death is near.
Fog and incense are all around me.

(M. Bojić, Unpublished Poem, Untitled)

For both Miss Todorović and Radivoje Bojić, the telegram informing them of the poet's death came as an unexpected shock. Bojić had written to his fiancée less than a month before his death, "I shall re-

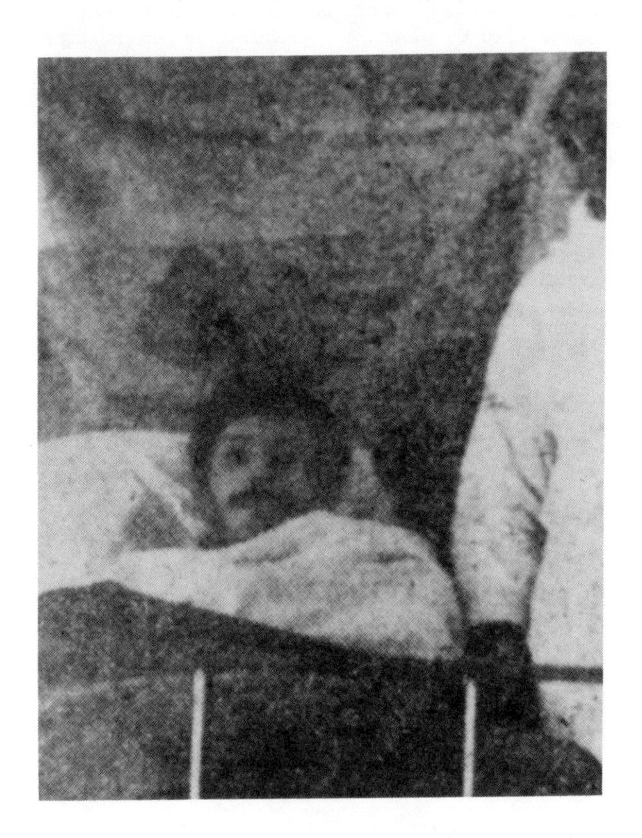

turn to you. . . . I shall come back. . . ."[19] And to his brother he had written, "I was slightly ill. Now I am on my way to recovery. I shall have a leave of convalescence and may be coming to France. . . ."[20]

On September 28, 1917, he wrote to his brother from the hospital, "Today I feel much better. One more week and I hope to be completely cured. . . ."[21] But on October 25, 1917, Bojić was dead. To the very last minute the poet had hoped to live, as is shown by a letter written by Milisav Janković, a patient in the same hospital, who, at the time, was even unaware that Bojić was a poet. As Janković wrote to his family, which had stayed in occupied Serbia,

---

19 Unpublished letter to Miss Todorović, dated September 1917.

20 Unpublished letter to Radivoje Bojić, dated September 1917.

21 *Ibid.*

> Three hours before his death, Bojić believed in his recovery and regularly asked the nurse for his medicine. He died choking in half-sleep from a fit of coughing that destroyed the tissues of his lungs.[22]

Milutin Bojić died on October 25, 1917, at the age of twenty-five, in the army hospital at Thessaloniki. He was buried in the military cemetery in Zejtinlik on October 27, 1917.

It was a cold, grey day, and the simple wooden crosses on the graves of the soldiers seemed lost in the fog. Only half of the cemetery was visible. Ivo Ćipiko, a well-known author, approached the tomb and began his eulogy with these words, "Poet of life and sunshine!"[23] While uttering these words, Ćipiko was shivering in the damp cold of this sad day.

Five years later, in October 1922, the remains of the poet were transferred to Belgrade and buried in the family vault. The inscription on the stone reads:

Jovan Bojić, 1854-1911
Sofija Bojić, 1865-1915
Jelica Nikolić, born Bojić, 1894-1942
Danica Bojić 1896-1952

A small distance away, to the right of the stone, is a stone plaque with a photograph of the poet and these words inscribed:

Give me the calm I need to find the strength
To give from my heart
All the suffering and the pride; this achieved
Let me fall as a dead leaf.

as well as a brief inscription

Milutin Bojić
Poet

---

[22] Unpublished letter, now belongs to Mrs. M. Janković.

[23] Details orally transmitted by Milisav Petrović, who was present at Bojic's funeral.

MILUTIN BOJIĆ, LYRIC POET

When we look at the poetry of Milutin Bojić, we immediately become aware of an apparent paradox. Bojić's most remarkable characteristic is his epic talent, and he was a visionary painter of tragic frescoes of epic grandeur. But he began as a lyric poet and remained a lyric poet through his entire career. In all his works, dramas and epos, Bojić always subjected all the facets of his art to lyrical emotionality. The strength of his dramas comes from their lyrical monologues. His historical dramas are today evocations of strong passions, and his characters are developed through emotional monologues, which are not based on a psychological study, but are depicted lyrically.

Bojić's emphasis on his lyrical sensitivity and its expression classified him as a pure romantic. If romanticism is, according to Emile Faguet, a predominance in art of emotion over reason and observation, then Bojić is a romantic with all the attendant vices and virtues. But his romanticism is much different from the romanticism of nineteenth century Serbian poetry, since it reflects a different social, cultural, and historic environment.

The proof is in the themes the poet selects, as well as in the way he treats them. The number of poetic themes in Bojić's work is rather restricted:

a) love – the woman as a symbol of sensuality and voluptuousness;
b) nationalism – as a result of the tragedy of World War I;
c) the vague longings and pains of adolescence.

The literary critic Dušan Milačić reduces Bojić's lyricism to "an orgy of voluptuousness and youth." The successive steps are "a hymn to the present; epicurianism; and a disregard for the future."[1] Milačić is right, but only partially. Bojić used these themes, but only during the first period of his artistic creativity, in his youth and before World War I. The fact that such poetry was unexpected in Serbia at the beginning of the twentieth century and that its form was impeccable account for the misunderstanding that labeled Bojić, once and for all, as a sensual poet, and this only on grounds of his youthful poems.[2] This interfered later with the emerging of a totally new lyric poet, as

---

1 Dušan Milačić: "M. Bojić, Lirski pesnik," *Misao*, Godina II, Sveska 10. 1920.

2 When Milačić wrote this article in 1920, he was unaware of Bojić's lyrical sonnets, which were published for the first time in 1922.

Bojić emerges in his later sonnets. These sonnets represent a purer sensuality and a new, lyrical spirituality.

An analysis of Bojić's lyrical poetry reveals two distinct periods of poetic creativity, stemming from two sources of superimposed inspiration, two different emotionalities. These poems come from two different periods of the poet's life, separated by the tragedy of war. Like two flowers that blossom on two separate branches of the same tree, his poems of uncontrolled youth are filled with young arrogance and vitality, but his love poems, written during the war, deal with the tragedy of exile, illness and death.

The second period is marked not only by a change of sensitivity. Bojić's inspiration also narrows down to two essential motifs: national tragedy and the rebirth of love, spiritualized through suffering. Love becomes tenderness and communion in suffering. These two themes represent the lyrical content both of the *Soneti* (Sonnets) and *Pesme Bola i Ponosa* (Poems of Suffering and Pride).

Bojić's first lyrical period comprises the poems published between 1910 and 1914. They are undoubtedly gifted, but they also bear the stamp of unmistakable adolescence and immaturity. Written by a young poet, between the ages of eighteen and twenty-two, these poems show a lack of balance and all the exaggerations that result from the chaotic emotions of the formative years. If the critic keeps this in mind, the exuberant vitality and spontaneity of the poems become even more appealing and are charming in a way that compensates for the lack of measure and harmony.

Because of the themes, these poems do not transcend the usual youthful emotions. But they represent an intensity of life and purity of form astounding in such a young poet. This sets them apart from other youthful attempts. They are already works of art, regardless of how young their author was.

In the first period of his lyric poetry, Bojić fully goes against the fashionable pessimism of his time. While Dis, Pandurović, and Svetislav Stefanović were lamenting the aimlessness and melancholy of life, the first poem Bojić published bears this significant title: *To Those Who Cry*. Though still naive in form, it clearly expresses the poet's attitude:

> I want to work, not to lose time,
> Not to complain later I had no luck,
> That my shoulders were weak under the burden,
> And that men were hard and cold as stone.
>
> (*Delo*, Knjiga 54, Sveska I, 1910)

Bojić's temperament at this point reflects his own youth. Thus, the characteristics of this phase of his lyrical poetry were:

a) a very personal sensuality, expressed with very little restraint;
b) a personal imagery that lent individual color to his sensations;
c) the pains and struggles of a passionate youth.

The poems of his early lyricism are hymns to sensuality. Passion is an exalted natural instinct that neither Bojić nor his Salome were able to fight. If we analyze this sensuality from a mature point of view, it might appear exaggerated, voluntarily tensed and forced to its ultimate limits. But if we remember our own adolescence, we recapture the meaning of such exaggerations, and our sensuality will emerge in our memory as it once was: natural and instinctive. Salome, when speaking of her sensuality, invokes nature itself:

Oh trees filled with perfume and resin
Your fruits taught me promiscuous passion!

(Salome, *Nova Iskra*, god. 10. br. 5. 1911)

This sensuality is not an individual sensuality created by a specific human being. It is something far larger, stronger, purer and more impersonal. It is the voice of passionate blood; it is the same sensuality that at the touch of Naksis's hand made the woods burst into bloom, with heavy, red flowers, as in Jovan Dučić's poem, *The Sap*.

The poems that Bojić dedicated to such a consuming passion are innumerable. During the first years of his artistic career he wrote: "I want you, oh life, and worship you. . . ." "You are the scorching noon of my sunny day. . . ". All his poetry in this period is an exaltation of boiling youth, a turmoil of young blood loaded with voluptuousness. His loves are those who in a kiss "drink the soul at the depth of a body." For him, "Youth is my god, and passion my strength." His entire credo consists of one word: passion. Concepts of morality, sin, virtue, do not exist for him. He only wants to hypnotize himself, to lose himself "in the eyes of bacchantes and nymphs." This involves no sacrifice of any idealized love, however, because at this stage nothing but physical sensations existed for the poet. It is a poetry of perfume and touch. But this physical sensitivity is given such an artistic form that it creates poems of spontaneous beauty. From an aesthetic standpoint, this theme, expressed with deep sincerity, is valid as any other. Furthermore, this aesthetic judgment should not be invluenced by the critic's personal ethical values—the morality or immorality of the theme have nothing to do with the intrinsic beauty of the work of art.

The second essential characteristic of this initial phase of Bojić's poetry is a very subjective and boundless lyricism. In the domain of love, a vast poetic domain whose slightest nuances poets have examined for centuries, Bojić does not roam widely. There is no interweaving of themes or graduated motives. The woman does not create a psychological process in the poet. Love is totally simplified inasmuch as it is reduced to pure sensuality. Bojić understands neither the intellectualism of symbolism nor the melancholy sweetness of romanticism. He is therefore estranged from the intimate shadings of love. The critics who search his poems for the nervousness and complications of the modern psyche or the pessimistic darkness of the poetry of the time simply do not find them. They do not realize that which the poet himself stressed: his poetry resembled a ripe fruit, warm in the sunshine, without sin, without nuances, but existing in the strong magnificence of nature itself. His poems do not express refined emotions or the complex shading of his inner life; they are essentially beautiful cries of victory in the vitality of passion.

Ctitics reproach him for having reduced the relationship of men and women to mere sensuality. This is an extremely delicate problem that, for centuries, has caused passionate disputes, which often ended in lawsuits against writers and poets. On one side, the fanatics of morality have tried to outlaw all erotic poetry. On the other, "the superior degenerates" and the "decadents" have tried to imbue aesthetics with impudence and vulgarity. But Bojić, though he published poems of total voluptuous spontaneity, never fell in the second category; the high artistic level of his work and his impersonal and healthy strength prevented him from doing so.

Though he uses a flamboyant rhetoric and at times a highly pompous verse, Bojić expresses a primitive passion and thus introduces a strong and overwhleming vitality into Serbian poetry. He is a strong and fresh wind that clears an atmosphere made heavy by poets who write under the complex and neurotic influence of foreign poetries. Bojić's poetry is far removed from the psychiatric wards. It is the poetry of a vigorous and passionate adolescent. Despite the definite influence of Baudelaire, Bojić never glorified sin, and his passions were never perverse.

Bojić never reacts in a way that can be loosely termed a "vice." He was never an alcoholic, though he enjoyed wine and occasionally used it in his poems to create a particular atmosphere. He does not even know drugs, the hasish of Baudelaire or Gauthier, the opium of Coleridge or De Quincey, the ether of Maupassant or Jean Lorain. His poetry, with all its sensuality and animalism, is young, healthy, and filled with vitality.

For the young Bojić, passion is the reason to live. But it is not a destructive passion as in Miloš Perović's poems ("Passion is a storm from which there is no shelter until it is over"). Nor is it stronger than conscience:

It flames boisterous and terrifying,
And brands with sin all that it reaches,
Destroys chastity, and in its place
Amidst a desert, reigns shame. . . .

(Miloš Perović, Passion)

Bojić's passion is completely natural, untouched by either shame or vice and unconcerned with consequences. Even when conscious of the desert that remains afterward, Bojić's passion is too elemental for him to think of it. Passion is not a vice that man tries desperately to avoid, and it is not a tragic and destructive storm. It is a simple and natural instinct discovered by a vigorous but dazed adolescent poet.

Bojić speaks of his sensuality openly, without recourse to subterfuge or fictional narratives. He trembles with passion and feels it in every drop of his blood, and it is so contained in every verse of his poems.

One of the essential characteristics of every lyric poet is that he places woman at the emotional focus of his world. The entire aesthetics of lyric poetry can be reduced, directly or indirectly, to the beauty of woman or the beauty of the emotion she creates in the poet. She is the *nervus rerum*, the driving force of all emotion. In lyric poetry she is the principle of all things.

To the woman belongs the crown
In the kingdom of beauty

(Bojić, Beauty)

To understand a poet's work, therefore, it is essential to understand his attitude toward woman. In Serbian poetry, as in all others, poets have seemingly exhausted all possible reactions to the beauty of the woman. She has been idealized until she has lost all her physical attributes; she has also been concretized physically until she has lost all moral consistency. Certain poets have loved the woman-soul, others the woman-female. Over-idealization has crippled the woman as much as has physical degradation. Few poets have found a balance, for equilibrium is essentially a non-poetic quality. Bojić's attitude in this respect was the logical consequence of his age and personality. He was young and handsome, he was prey to his vitality and temperament, women loved him, and his temptations were numerous. He learned spontaneously to know the physical woman, the sensual woman, because it was this woman who attracted him and whom he attracted. She inspired his sensual poems during the first phase of his artistic career.

In lyric poetry, the woman reflects the poet's own personality. An essentially sensual poet will create a voluptuous woman, while a melancholy poet will create an idealized and dreamlike woman, with whom he can lament on the sadness of being alive.

The most frequent type of sensual woman in poetry is the woman who is both sensual and mystical at the same time. For example, Baudelaire's mistresses incorporate in one woman the temptation of sin and the suffering of remorse. However, in German poetry, the sensual woman is more frequently devoid of any mysticism and is the mere object of the poet's passion. This is the case with the sensual woman who emerged from a combination of naturalism and individualism and who is the central figure of several poems by Lilienkron. This type is very akin to the demoniac woman in the romantic poetry of the nineteenth century, but it has an added touch of modernistic neurosis.

The woman Bojić celebrated in his early poems is neither demoniac nor mystically sinful. She, like the poet, is dominated by the desire to live fully through the senses. But there is no gloom of fatality, no conflict between sin and conscience. She is no mere object for the poet's sensuality; they are both voluptuaries.

> Intoxicated with hatred, surrounded by screams,
> In a sensual kiss our bleeding lips are glued,
> And strong ribs strain under the pressure
> Of unconscious fingers that grip them with passion.
>
> (M. Bojić, The Kiss, 1912)

Bojić also exhibits another characteristic of adolescence: he splits the image of woman into two parts. The perception of woman in two separate categories, the idealized woman and the brutally materialized woman, is a frequent result of youthful sexual awakening. On one side are the purely sensual and physical desires, and on the other, the erotic sublimation into the psychological domain and their appearance in the form of a mystical crisis, as well as the suffering of the adolescent struggle to achieve adulthood. Sexual desire, temperament, milieu, religion, the intensity of intellectual life all will play an important role in the formation and expression of a young poet's sensuality. In the case of Bojić, his sensuality was never subjected to outside pressures and, thus, he did not hesitate to give it full and spontaneous expression. On the contrary, with all the exaggeration of an adolescent, he elevated sensuality to the level of a personal religion. He tells us this straightforwardly in the poem *The Hymn*, which contains the credo of his early youth:

I want you life, and respect you deeply!
I was born to be a prophet of the young
Who will want you strongly with a serene brow.

Then I shall drink the requiem of virtue
And drink avidly with parted lips
Delights, delights, delights, deep and endless.

(M. Bojić, The Hymn, 1911)

This is the concept of love that Bojić expressed in the first collection of his poems, published in 1914, before he witnessed the sacrifices his people had to make every day during the war. All this was before he became the poet of national tragedy and pride.

In these adolescent poems, Bojić glorified life and its sensual pleasures. If it can be said that Zola wrote a pessimistic epos on "human animality," then it can just as well be stated that Bojic wrote a lyrical panegyric on "optimistic animality." He classified emotions as pleasant or unpleasant, not as good or bad. This is yet another sign of moral immaturity.

But he is not the only Serbian poet of his time to sing healthy, vigorous and sensual love. Another poet, a Dalmatian, Mirko Korolija, who is as exalted temperamentally as Bojić, seems to rival his ardent coloring of themes and verses. Korolija's collected poems were published in the same year, 1914, and show the same impulsiveness, pantheism, and thirst for life. We will refer to this in a later chapter dealing with mutual influences among contemporary poets.

Bojić is at the opposite pole from the poet Dučić. For Dučić, woman is a mystery, the inspiration for all things, the essential reason for all joy and suffering. For Bojić, woman is the generator of all inner emotions.

If we compare two poems by Dučić and Bojić concerning the image of the woman, the difference becomes even more evident:

Oh, goddess who, proud and fierce,
From vast and unknown crossroads
First came into man's sight,
Holding your breats in your hands—

And sounded in the twilight of the first dawn
Your bloodthirsty laughter, while the hot
Torch of the sun still slept in the woods.

The eyes of all things looked up to you,
The lily in the big garden copied you,
And the sun came to burn in your hair;
Pale marble wanted your strange lines.

(Jovan Dučić, Poem to the Woman)

Sleepy earth breathed its purple vapors,
Blue evergreens lowered their heads,
Over dead seas crows were crying sadly,
The Southern sun was melting in a golden bronze.

The burning sand glared and shimmered;
Tearing the skies, tall mountains slept;
On the red beach dreamed a flock of cranes,
Flies were dancing over the river.

Hot, drowsy, in the music of peace and colors,
Bored, man watched this luxury.
He lay bloody, a mess of hair and sweat,
And tried to see himself in the sunny rays.

The ripe hour of the day was empty.
Men waited for a form new,
A thing lush, sunny, like sea foam.
Suddenly he laughed with throaty passion.

Down evergreen slopes came the woman.

(M. Bojić, The Legend of the Woman)

These two poems reveal completely different concepts of woman. For Bojić, her sole importance is that she causes passion to erupt. She thus gives a meaning to the physical life of the primitive man. This was Bojić's first concept of love, and it was difficult at the time to conceive that he, of all Serbian poets, would pay the greatest praise to women—in his poem *Žene* (Women). Some deep tragedy must have brought the poet of *The Legend of the Woman* to the verses in *Women*:

In a graveyard a group of prowling women
Treads silently not to wake the dead;
In long lines they string yellow candles:
Winter winds howl over the city.

(M. Bojić, Women, 1916)

In Bojić's first poetry, published in 1914, there are also poems dedicated to the turmoils of adolescence. When the young man is forced to break with the world of his childhood, when he ceases to accept the world without evaluation, Bojić wrote some poems in which he captured the sufferings and hesitations of youth. Three of these poems: *Vrane* (The Crows), *Mladost* (The Youth), and *Hod* (The Marching), are milestones on his road from childhood to maturity. They recall the turmoil that we felt in our youth but that we forgot when the years deadened these emotions. For this reason, these poems by Bojić still remain favorites with the young, who feel the poems belong to them, and who view Bojić as a poet of the young. And these young people are right.

The Crows, one of Bojić's first published poems, is an introduction to the problems of youth. It is a poetic expression of the painful moment when an adolescent feels for the first time that his relationship with the outside world is no longer a logical one. Everything around him is deformed because it is filtered through the prism of an unformed personality. One of the first experiences of this ego, as it undergoes a painful birth, is the anxiety felt when one no longer belongs to the mass of amorphous beings among whom the child felt at ease. It is the first awareness that every human being is an entity unto itself. The adolescent faces a new world and a series of entirely new value problems. This world is exclusively his, and this exclusive ownership makes him aware of the enormous gap that divides him from "the others." One of the first consequences of this new attitude is a feeling of poignant and total loneliness. This loneliness creates a desire to be understood, as well as a need to reconstruct, on one's own terms, a world that has collapsed. In a word, these are the well-known vague desires that express themselves in aimless suffering.

These emotions are clearly expressed in *The Crows*, which deserves to be quoted in its entirety, as is is quite characteristic of Bojić's youthful poetry.

> For a long time I watched the crows flying,
> Black as youth falling into an abyss.
> Far away the west flared at moments,
> Under grey clouds hunted by the wind.
> Without sound or aim the crows flew.
> Black, all equal, they told the tragic story—
> How terrifying it is to resemble the others.
> Silence: mortals and eternity struggle.
> The world around me falls into their net.
> How terrifying it is to resemble the others!
> A cry, bursting with passion, tore the night.
> The voice of a crow. The flock rushed after him.
> And he cried, conscious of his powers,
> And led his black brothers to their goal.
> Soundlessly the crows flew through the night.
> I shivered and felt at that moment
> I resembled an unknown chaste woman
> Who, stepping on the path that leads to her downfall,
> Shudders, while shame flushes her face.
> That night my will was born in me.
>
> (M. Bojić, The Crows)

If the poem is analyzed verse by verse, following the method of Bogdan Popović, the first element is a visual representation of nature. But it is a typically romantic adaptation of nature to fit the poet's emotions, not an objective aesthetic appreciation of a landscape. The identification of nature and the poet's ego, in which nature meshes with the inner emotion that triggered the poem, is an essential characteristic of the very young romantic poet. And Bojić is both: young and romantic. In the first stanza the words "at moments" identify nature and the ego. At sunset, the sky does not flare "at moments," but the young poet's emotions do.

"Without a sound, without an aim, the crows flew" is a symbolic evocation of the poet's still aimless youth. In his formative years, Bojić shied away from a precise aim, which would circumscribe his freedom within a complete, concrete ego. The repetitive motive: "How terrible it is to resemble the others" is an affirmation of the individualism already mentioned. It is also a negation of the annihilated world of childhood, the world of non-individualistic and impersonal values. It is a world in which emotions are distinguished only by their intensity and not their values. A child as a rule finds his similarity to all the others comfortable and suffers if he is pointed out as different. The acceptance of personal identity is the rejection of childhood.

In his next poem, *The Marching*, Bojić rejects his childhood even more clearly:

> I laugh now at what childhood deplores,
> Those pale days of handed-down thought,
> Vague sorrows and unconscious longings:
> Great was the day when our soul fell.
>
> (M. Bojić, The Marching)

Thus, *The Crows* reflects Bojić's discovery of the ego, while *The Marching* is a more evolved form of the struggle for individuality. *The Crows* has a premonition of a powerful passion, the force of nature that leads the black crows. But sensual voluptuousness is still missing and will become an essential characteristic only in the later poems. *The Crows* also contains a sense of danger, hesitation, and shame. It is a diagram, as it were, of the first phase of the poet's self-discovery.

The Youth, which was written a short time later, no longer reflects the initial phase, since the struggle for individuality has already progressed and is evident in the abstract suffering and the still vague desires.

The first verses of the poem are the very image of youth:

> All I know is I want, but not what I want,
> A thousand things at the same time. . .
>
> (M. Bojić, The Youth)

The poem has all the imprecision of an unconscious desire, and it later confesses that the suffering tearing at the poet's soul has no specific cause. It is the result of the search for harmony between objective reality and the formation of the personality, as Bojić makes clear in two separate verses:

> Insane with suffering, but not unhappy. . .
> . . . .
> and drive from his breast this pain that hurts not. . .
> . . . .

Though extremely young, Bojić already knows how to concentrate the precise image of an imprecise suffering in only a few words. "Insane with suffering, but not unhappy" describes the phase of youth when suffering is not yet the logical effect of a personal and practical cause. Youth almost takes pleasure in aimless suffering, and we will never find a better description than Bojić's "a pain that hurts not."

Vladimir-Velmar Janković[3] treats Bojić's poems in a completely different way: "Bojić expresses his sensuality with the boldness of an adolescent straining with his first desires and for whom puberty has no suffering nor fears of his instincts." It seems that Janković either failed to notice Bojić's youthful poems, or failed to understand them.

But in July of 1910, Bojić already rationalizes his feelings. The initial struggle is over:

> And ripened youth is looking for a goal,
> Striving from the soul, heart, breast,
> Even pain is welcome, when it irritates,
> For her to rave, to suffer, exasperated, insane.
>
> (M. Bojić, Youth)

Written in 1912, barely two years after *The Crows*, the poem *The Marching* is already a compromise. The young poet has come to terms with life. He seeks inner harmony, though he has not yet achieved it. Pessimism and suffering remain, but they now stem from the distance that separates the idealized dreams of youth from the concrete realities of life.

---

[3]Velmar J[illegible]ković, M. Bojić, "Pesme i Drame," *Novi Vidici*, God. I. broj. 1, 1928.

Bojić becomes aware of the relativity of emotions, of the fact that his beliefs belong only to himself and are a manifestation of his newfound ego.

> We believe bravely to the last moment
> For upon our strings the psalm is played.
>
> (M. Bojić, The Marching)

Once he has understood and accepted his own uniqueness and the terrible loneliness this entails, Bojić has left the struggles of adolescence, that period in which he had wants and desires but was unable to identify precisely what these wants and desires were.

The period that saw the first publication of Bojić's poems is marked by a wave of pessimism in Serbian poetry, and this literary milieu undoubtedly influenced his first works. But pessimism was alien to the vigorous temperament of the young poet. He freed himself very rapidly and turned to a very sensual romanticism. Thus, Bojić took a position in Serbian poetry far from the philosophical pessimism of the German *Weltanschauung* and far from the intimate pessimism of Rajić.

Although Bojić was by no means an intellectual poet, which would be surprising at the age of eighteen, he tried his hand at intellectual poetry. These are his weak poems. When he forced his talent in the direction of philosophical, abstract, pessimistic poetry, instead of expressing his own violent and youthful emotions, the result was mostly confusion. The wealth of his vocabulary and the metallic rhythm of his verse that is so enchanting when he sings of passion suddenly sound empty, and the stultified insincerity is cloying. Unfortunately, in this first period of his career, his youth made him believe a tribute should be paid to his literary environment.

Fortunately, such poems are rare. The more frequent pessimism is the sadness of youth, which we have just analyzed.

In 1912, Bojić wrote "Razejane Vatre" and "Herostrati." These two poems have the same pessimistic outlook found in Rakić's *Sonet I*. But Rakić, a much more mature and formed poet at the time, writes of the inescapable flow of time, of old age and death inevitably coming to point out the futility of all our efforts and destroy all our achievements. In the twenty-year-old Bojić, such poems are only exercises in versification. Because of his youth and his ardent love of life, such feelings are out of his reach.

> Cruel time will destroy all our works,
> Be they written by pen, gun, or sword,
> Slowly, inevitably, they will be ground,
> In the inescapable mill of death.
>
> (M. Rakić, Sonnet I)

It is the constant story of the same pain,
Clad in the same cloud of temptation,
The astronomer searches a source of salvation,
Then, weak, sits and waits for the day of his death.
(M. Bojić, Scattered Flames)

Filled with rhetorical flourishes, Bojić's poem does not sound sincere. It sounds more like scale exercises at the piano. When he needed poetic practice, Bojić took what themes were available—from the fashionable pessimism of his time. But these themes remained foreign to him, though, at times, he would begin a poem as a study in versification and then succumb to the emotion of the theme. Then the poem would rise on wings of spontaneous inspiration and become a true work of art.

The poem *Herostrati* begins with the theme of the frailty of earthly endeavors, but the pompous tone of the opening verses soon fades, and each line rings more and more true. In the sixth stanza Bojić achieves such spontaneity and beauty of expression that it becomes one of the best poems of this entire collection. Gradually the poem moves, almost imperceptibly, from philosophy into the emotions, a domain that is entirely Bojić's.

A freezing wind blows over our heads;
In vain our chisels and long lasting efforts;
There is nothing for us even to demolish,
Our temples, even, others have demolished.

We cry when midnight darkens our eyes,
Ashamed to die alone without any wreath,
And, with pain, we build huge shrines,
Only to burn them with our own hands.
(M. Bojić, Herostrati)

These two stanzas are among the best in the 1914 collection. They express the poet's youthful idealism and his need to achieve something great, as well as the adolescent fear that everything great had already been done and said.

Sincere and spontaneous, as a work of art *Deus Deorum* ranks with *Herostrati*. It has a feeling of transcendence from individual to collective emotion, which is mostly achieved by quoting illustrious names from the past. And many beautiful poetic images are scattered throughout the poem.

In the Pantheon the clapping of your hands,
Was the applause to the work of spiders. . .

Or, in the same vein,

When midnight deadens streets and palaces,
You guard, crouched, the dark and empty forum,
Debasing idols, spitting on dead warriors,
You eternal doubt, you Deus Deorum.

Bojić gives here a very poetic description of the suffering caused by the embrace of doubt, of which it could be said, as Rakić said for the embrace of thought, that "it crushes bones and opens wounds."

But even though he wrote pessimistic poems, Bojić is neither a philosophical nor pessimistic poet. When he touched these themes (and he did so only in several of his youthful poems), it was mostly because of literary fashion. Had he continued this way, he would probably have remained only a gifted disciple of other great poets. But he was able to express his youthful and sensual vitality spontaneously and poetically, and his first collection of poems was an original and new contribution to Serbian poetry.

Bojić's later love poems—his sonnets—are totally different from his earlier poems. He had suffered through the Albanian exodus, and the young poet who previously exalted life had become the patriotic poet of his nation's sufferings. In his lyrical poems, his concepts of love are totally different. In their emotional tone, the Sonnets do not resemble at all Bojic's youthful poetry. The poet had matured incredibly rapidly and was to die young, like Shelley and André Chenier.[4]

In his early poems, Bojic denied woman any human quality, in a spontaneous though forced expression of sensuality. In the period of war and tragedy, his emotions became spiritualized, transposed, deeply human. His emotions came to center on the love of one woman. His feelings became warm, harmonious, tender. We have no intention of belittling his first poems, for such a reproach would be as illogical as resenting the fact that Hérédia has the sculptural beauty of marble instead of the musical fluidity of the symbolists. Every poet searches for spontaneous expression of his sincere feelings, and a change in emotions leads to a change in poetry. The only important question is the artistic worth of his work. The rest remains part of the poet's personality. Dučić's poetry is aristocratic, Rakić's spiritual, Santić's warm and human, Luković's elegaic, and Bojić's, in his first period, sensual, and in the second, spiritual and almost

[4] The Sonnets were published only in 1922, five years after the death of the poet. They were not written for publication. They were neither polished nor prepared for publication. They are in the form he sent to his fiancée, Miss Todorović, who was then a refugee in France. There are thirty-two sonnets, numbered I to XXXII.

humble. This must be said, since many Serbian literary critics. such as Milačić, Novaković, and Janković, find an emotional superficiality in Bojić's poetry. They constantly repeat that Bojić lacked inner intuition and the subtlety of "soul language." As Novaković writes: "If we need poets who address themselves to our soul, we will not find this in Bojić; he is nothing but one of the small ones."[5] Though Bojić does not speak to our soul in his first collection of verses, we can but wonder whether Novaković ever read his Sonnets.

The Sonnets express the poet's sincere and personal love and indeed reach the soul of the reader. Their themes are much more varied than those of the first youthful poems and encompass a broad scale of human emotions. A deep change has occurred in the soul of the poet. The woman has become a human being, the inspirer, the merciful consoler, almost a mystery of idealization:

> Fade away, thus, translucent and dreamy
> For me to remember always the same:
> As an icon to protect me from all evil.
>
> (Sonnet III)

> In you I want to hide my sufferings,
> And, different from the man everybody knows,
> On your breast, as on my native soil,
> Hidden from others, I want to cry.
> . . . .
> . . . .
> . . . .
> Then I shall return pure to a world of filth,
> Return with no sin nor suffering.
> Oh, be my church and my saving god!
>
> (Sonnet XXI)

This concept of love is diametrically opposed to the concept of love in Bojić's first poems. Woman has become the meaning and savior of man. She gives value to things, she shelters, and she ultimately redeems.

Bojić's Sonnets were written during the tragic years of war, at the same time as his Poems of Suffering and Pride. Past temptations have now become futile, though at times the poet regrets them and tries to recapture them. He wishes to dive again into the meaningless joy of past sensual days, but realizes that it is impossible in the face of suffering. Careless youth is dead, for him as well as in him. Once passion was in every drop of his blood; now he suffers for his people.

> I cannot even sin as I used to sin before . . .
>
> (M. Bojić, Sonnet XVI)

[5] Boško Novaković, "Poezija Milutina Bojića," *Misao*, Knjiga 49, Sveska 1-4, September-October 1932.

Foreign you are, foreign, my nights . . .
(M. Bojić, Sonnet XXIX)

Not only is the poet unable to abandon himself to the passion and youthful vitality of bygone days, but sensual accents are also very rare in his verses. The words "sadness" and "sorrow," which do not appear in his first poems, occur more and more frequently in his sonnets.

Every poet has his favorite word. As Vladimir Ćorović notes so well in his *Foreword* to Bojic's *Poems and Dramas*, for Heinrich Heine it is "pain," for Baudelaire "sickness," and for Bojic "blood" in the first period, and "sadness" in the second. This collection of poems is no longer, as Bojić used to say of his first works, "The hot noon of a burning summer day." It is the poet's sad twilight.

While the red twilight sings to ripe fruit,
And I hide my desperate loneliness . . .
(M. Bojić, Sonnet XXV)

A foreboding of approaching death, a painful twilight for a twenty-five year old poet—these are the essential emotions of the Sonnets. This new tone recurs in words like "languid," "painful," and "autumnal sadness." It seems difficult to believe that only several years have so completely changed the author of *Griphos* that he now writes:

And let your beautiful face dampen
My mad rushing and stop it, caress it gently
And chase it far, far away.

And while your eyes get larger,
And perfumes envelop you,
May you hear my soul, full of sadness.
(M. Bojić, Sonnet XXII)

For the poet, everything has now acquired the bitter charm of memories. All that he loves is gone: his country, his home, freedom, and family. Why be surprised by the deep sadness of these verses, even if they were written by a young man, and even if that young man once was the sensual poet Milutin Bojić? He no longer asks from life "delights, delights, deep and endless . . . ," but:

Only a new Christ full of mercy,
To shed my tears in his embrace.
(M. Bojić, Sonnet XXVI)

But if this sadness is natural and understandable, it is nonetheless surprising that most literary critics did not notice it. Bojić's Sonnets are rarely mentioned, because Bojić's image as an exclusively sensual poet was too firmly established in the minds of the critics. None noticed the new lyrical tone of the Sonnets, and, for the critics, Bojić has always remained the poet of the animalistic joy of life.

It is not easy to die even when life is a tragedy and all hope seems futile, but it is even harder when one is young and the soul still young and passionate. In these moments Bojić achieves the pathos of Branko Radičević and finally depicts the nuances of inner life that critics have found lacking in his work (Velmar Janković). Bojić wrote admirably on the suffering of death at twenty-five, as he came to understand the inevitability of one's death. The poet who in his youth wanted to "drink life," who was a hawk drunk with blood, now writes verses that are pathetic in their suffering:

> Oh, my poor lilies and tulips,
> Bend your heads, the time has come to wilt,
> Never will you again at dawn
> Hear the shouts of laughter and joy.
> . . . .
> . . . .
> In the past you called me with perfumes
> And offered your petals to my kisses
> At moments when sounds and colors hug.
> Now there is sadness all around us,
> Oh, my poor lilies and tulips,
> No more is there sun. It is time to wilt.
> (M. Bojić, Sonnet XXVIII)

The brief war between Serbia and Turkey in 1912 brought the first patriotic motifs celebrating the victory of Serbia. In 1913, Bojić wrote his first patriotic poetry, which was included in the collection published in 1914. They are still exaggeratedly romantic poems and take in a broad range of pathos, since Bojić was here attempting to emulate Victor Hugo's rhetorical verse. In the few patriotic poems he wrote during this period, Bojić was still searching for an original artistic expression. He needed grandeur, which he found during the tragic year 1915. Nevertheless, these first patriotic poems already presage the magnificent coloring of Bojić's later poems and announce the arrival of the future poet of *Poems of Suffering and Pride*.

The first patriotic poem in the 1914 collection is entitled *Zemlja Oluje*[6] (The Country of Storms), which had been published separately, just prior to the 1912 Serbo-Turk War. It is still rather impersonal in tonality and does not give the impression that the poet had lived it in depth. It strikes us rather as an exercise on a contemporary theme, composed under the influence of the literary milieu. *Zemlja Oluje* is

---

6 "Zemlja Oluje," *Srpski Književni Glasnik*, Knjiga XXIX, sveska 9, November, 1912.

a poem of tense and exalted romanticism, but it is important for the analysis of Bojić's further development, since it is his first step in a new direction. As through a veil, the future poet of the grandiose *Sejači* can be seen in some of its verses.

During the Balkan wars of 1912 and 1913, Bojić published in *Srpski Književni Glasnik* a whole series of patriotic poems under the general title *Himna Pokoljenja* (Hymn of Generations). They are subtitled *Vaskrs* (Ressurection), *Hod* (The Marching), *Razmah* (The Effort), *Spomen* (The Remembrance), *Fanfare* (The Trumpets), and *Grobovi* (The Tombs).

Much better artistically than the poems in *Hymn of Generations*, however, is a poem that, though it was written at the same time, is not included in this collection. It is entitled *Poslednji Imperator* (The Last Emperor). Even thoug its structure is still unbalanced, and even though the emotion, and even the meaning, are often sacrificed to the sound effect of words, the poem is a striking example of the Parnassian movement's influence on the Serbian poetry of Bojić's time. Bojić often uses the French technique, in which the end of a poem does not close the thought but seems to open new horizons; here the influence of Jose-Maria de Hérédia is apparent. In most Serbian poets, this influence is indirect. It reached them through Dučić, one of the strongest propagators of French influence in Serbian poetry. The last few verses in Bojić's *Last Emperor* reflect Dučić's *Imperial Sonnet*, which in turn reflects the conclusion of Hérédia's sonnet *Anthony and Cleopatra*.

The Emperor, lowering his sword, watched
New generations march through deep valleys.
(M. Bojić, The Last Emperor)

And with closed eyes, lying on fur and silk,
The Emperor saw, crossing the high vault,
The ghost of Nemanja in triumphant march.
(J. Dučić, Imperial Sonnet)

Bent over her, the ardent Emperor,
Saw in her eyes, studded with golden stars,
A vast sea where ships were fleeing.
(J.-M. de Hérédia, Anthony and Cleopatra)

The patriotic themes in Bojić's poetry appear more and more frequently after 1914, until, by 1917, all other themes disappear, all others, that is, except for the spiritual and deep love for his fiancée, Miss Todorović. This he expressed in the *Sonnets* he sent her while she was in France.

Bojić published his *Poems of Suffering and Pride* just before his death, when he was already exhausted by physical and moral pain.

This collection contains his best patriotic poems and reflects the great national tragedy through which he lived in his final years. These are also his best-known poems, without which any anthology of Serbian poetry would be incomplete.

For his patriotic poems, Bojić chose a style in almost complete contrast to the one he used in his love poems. In the romantic love poetry he published in 1914, the *I* is always present, since it reflects his entirely subjective lyricism. This personal *I* disappears completely in his patriotic poetry, giving way to the suffering of a whole nation, in comparison with which the poet's personal emotions and sacrifice are of little importance. Thus, Bojić concerned himself neither with his personal tragedy nor with that of individual human beings caught in the destruction of an entire nation. His was not the individual approach of Arthur Rimbaud's *Dormeur du Val* nor that of a soldier's letter as in V. Ilić's *Vojničko Pismo* (A Soldier's Letter). Bojić, as a man, fades away before the vastness of the tragedy. His poems do not express the personal awe, admiration, and suffering of Milutin Bojić facing the destruction of his country and nation; they express the will and sacrifice of that entire nation. This is a rare achievement for so young a poet.

Two motifs constantly reappear during these years: the Albanian exodus and the exile in Thessaloniki. The exodus was a retreat before an all-powerful enemy, the abandonment of country, home, and family for a forced march through the snow and ice-covered mountains to Greece. Thessaloniki represents a new hope, which, "like a new wind." speaks of rebirth and victory. If the exodus is the deathly darkness closing in on the country, the exile is the first ray of a new dawn.

Bojić painted a vast fresco of those heroic days. While Filipović, Jelić, and Milutin Jovanović dedicated their poems to the death of individual heroes and personal losses, Bojić spoke of his country and people. As a result of his exaltation and his epic qualities, he managed to avoid the monotony that could easily have marred his collection. It is extremely difficult for a poet to build an entire collection of poems on one motif, even if the motif is awe-inspiring. But Bojić was able to compose a whole collection of poems on this one theme, without falling prey to monotony and repetition.

Poems of Suffering and Pride is composed of thirty-five poems, of which only twenty-nine are published in the edition of *Srpska Književna Zadruga*. This edition is the only one available, since the original burned in the great fire of Thessaloniki in 1917. The poems in the published collection have an epic quality suited to the tragedy of the time,

Through winter midnights, through storms of despair,
Through winds and mountains, snows and waters,
You march silently, to meet your fate,
You march silently, my enslaved people.
(M. Bojić, The Departure)

As if facing the gates of old Canaan
A nation stands that refused temptation,
Stern as the Cedars of antique Lebanon,
Calm as a congregation at a solemn mass.
(M. Bojić, Before the Promised Land)

The same power of personification is apparent in the poem *Žene* (The Women), where the poet evokes a vision of the mothers, the wives, and the sisters who stayed in occupied Serbia to tend the graves and who thus link the tragic past and the hope of a victorious future.

Petrified and mute they face the crosses
Night and cold creep into their bones.
(M. Bojić, Women)

At this point, the romantic *I* of the love poems had ceased to exist, and the poet plumbs the depth of collective suffering. The exalted tone caused by the sublime vision of national pride and suffering becomes stronger through the collection of poems, until it culminates in the poem *Krštenje Večnosti* (Baptism of Eternity), the vast image that symbolizes the grandeur of the tragedy. It expresses the concept of a nation's sacrifice, consciously accepted and paid in order to continue living its own ideal of freedom and national identity. The motif is the same as in Alfred de Vigny's poem *Moses*—pride in self-imposed sacrifice for an ideal. The Serbian nation, like Vigny's Moses, wanted only "the peace of calm days." It is not given to fanaticism nor the spirit of earthly conquests, but it resorts to war, self-sacrifice, and cruel extermination in order to preserve a high ideal.

At a midnight, through sounds and fury,
For a moment Eternity gazed, wtih fiery eyes,
At my people. All they wanted was humble peace.
From that gaze they shrink, like a wilted flower.

And the voice said: "You are the chosen ones!
You were not born for peaceful acceptance,
But for vast and endless summits!
I shall baptize you with waters of grandeur!"
(M. Bojić, Baptism of Eternity)

The freedom of the country is a sacred national heritage. Bojic sees the Serbian nation as an eternal sentinel, and Serbia's glory comes from its people's eternal willingness to die for their freedom.

The fate of this people was decided the day they came to live on this soil:

> For each step must be sacred through death,
> And the tear-soaked soil covered with blood.
> (M. Bojić, Baptism of Eternity)

From this essential idea springs the vision of these poems, the vast vision that eradicates all the personal emotions of the poet. These poems are huge images, painted with strong brush-strokes, which, by their tragic horror, are reminiscent of Dante's *Inferno*. For example, the title of the poem, *Sejači* (The Sowers) brings to mind peaceful peasants planting their fields. But for Bojić, these same humble farmers, instead of planting corn on peaceful fields, are planting their very own bones, which have been scattered in exile:

> But still we sow our bones lavishly
> Through islands and foreign waters,
> Through deserts and howling simoons,
> And frozen steppes. And at eventide
> Gorged with blood vultures leave our bodies.
> (M. Bojić, The Sowers)

The image evoked is one of sacred terror, and the last stanza, identical to the first except for one verse, carries the meaning to a peak:

> Proud, though we have no kinfolk nor roof:
> Intrepid we shall face new cemeteries.
> (M. Bojić, The Sowers)

The tragedy of an entire nation is captured in two short lines. They express the pride and the sacrifice of a young nation, which had the strength to rise from its own ashes.

To sing of those tragic days, Bojić turned spontaneously to the Bible, which he had studied extensively before the war. At times he addressed God directly in his prayers, as in the poem *Nerečene Misli*, or at times in involuntary blasphemy, when pain is unbearably strong, as in *Vera*. But in all cases he went back to the majestic, rhythmic imagery of the Bible.

The poem *Nerečene Misli* (Untold Thoughts) reminds us of the most poetic passages of the Bible. Condensed in its hallucinatory grief, it is one of the most beautiful of Bojić's poems. Only rarely can a poet attain such sublime heights. Unfortunately, the poem lacks polish. But if it were not for several weak verses, it would undoubtedly be one of the greatest works of art in Serbian poetry:

Oh, God of my fathers, Lord of my children,
Why abandon me and destroy all I had?
Our churches toll dead instead of hours,
And at your altar my heart is bleeding.

. . . .
. . . .

Oh, God of my fathers, do you see my daughters?
For the feats of enemies they are like fruit and wine:
If I have sinned, let not their chastity atone;
Cover with plague their breasts and lips,
Make them hideous so that their pure bodies
Don't serve as drinking cups to the enemy.
(M. Bojić, Untold Thoughts)

Bojić had the visionary gift of embracing vast perspectives, out of which came his two great poems *Petrovdanska vizija* and *Plava Grobnica*. The first was written for St. Peter's Day (King Peter I) and subsequently became one of the strongest poems in this collection.[7]

From the poem's very beginning, the atmosphere recalls Elsinor Castle, where, more real than reality, roam ghosts of doubts and truths and struggles and surrenders-to-fate. It is another world, in which the tragic, white-haired King Peter meets the ghost of the medieval Despot. The vision is told in verses worthy of the world's best epic poems.

Then, pale as a midnight cobweb,
With his long beard, with his hand on his sword,
Wearing his crown and royal red gown,
With majestic attitude, the Despot met him and said:

. . . .
. . . .

I heard women sob at their obscene feasts,
And children scream, pierced by their swords,
I heard an entire nation that lamented.
Over blood boiling in their enemy's cups.

. . . .
. . . .

Both our faces are marked by suffering,
Our fates are similar, though their ends differ:
Your tortured people march to Palm Sundays,
Mine were rewarded by their Good Friday.
(M. Bojić, The Vision on Saint Peter's Day)

---

[7] *Petrovdanska Vizija* (The Vision on Saint Peter's Day) was first published in *Srpske Novine*, number 35, June 29, 1916, on the island of Corfu.

In this poem Bojić creates characters who, through their epic despair and the depth of their tragedy, call Shakespeare to mind. The Despot, Djuradj Branković, is suffering personified. He lost his throne and country to the Turks, and his son was blinded. But in Bojić's vision, the ghost of the Despot summons the strength to utter words of hope. The Despot and the King appear before our darkened eyes in a slow but majestic walk, as do centuries of suffering and millions of dead heroes. As inexorable as Jehovah, Fate is looking for the man most worthy to be crowned with suffering and glory.

Bojić, a romantic poet who glorified the nation and forgot the humble individual martyr, is a visionary. But his romanticism is more real than isolated cases of realism. In certain instances, there are reflections of human weakness, and they suddenly make the poet a single suffering man. From verses that seem sculpted in the marble of petrified tragedy, he suddenly turns to other tones of sorrow:

> My Lord, forgive me my moment of weakness,
> For then I heard the nostalgic whisper,
> From my mountain of pines and evergreens,
> Crushed and age old, my forests cursed me.
>
> (M. Bojić, The Temple)

The poem *Molitva* (A Prayer), though it appears in the 1914 collection, belongs to *Pesme Bola i Ponosa* in both tone and form. It was written in 1911, but it appears, and rightfully so, in the later collection published by *Srpska Književna Zadruga*. It is another example of tenderness and human sadness, of sorrow without words or tears. It contains the essential Serbian tradition of Kossovo, the concept that one does not fight wars to conquer empires and lose one's soul. It is not a war of hatred, but a war to save national freedom and the right to worship one's God. The words "hatred" or "revenge" do not appear once in this collection. War is for Bojić a national sacrifice for the ideal of freedom. But the poet needs vast spaces and grandiose paintings to depict terrible sufferings. Artistically, he reverts to the epics of Serbian folklore and rejects the balance of moderation. Like Hugo, he sings of Titans, and it is only in this vastness larger than nature that he is natural. Bojić is also aware that a nation's greatness does not lie solely in battlefields, but in works of art as well. He therefore aspired to be the poet who would transpose in poems the ideas of Serbian martyrdom. In some of his poems, he achieved this goal.

It would be necessary to relive the tragedy that followed the Albanian exodus in order to feel the full impact of *Plava Grobnica* (The Sea Grave). As if crucified on the cross of national tragedy, Bojić reaches higher and higher levels of emotion, until the summit,

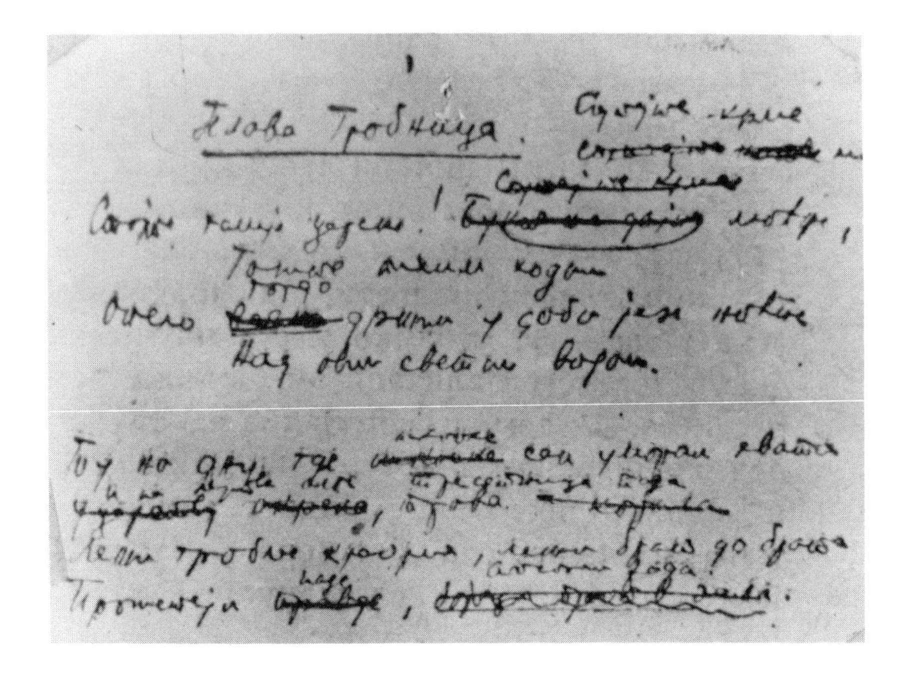

Плава Гробница

Fragment of Bojić's handwritten draft of *Plava Grobnica.*

where the petty ceases to exist, even pride, even suffering, and where all that remains is the feeling of duty accomplished, of sacrifice in the name of freedom. Once he reached this height, he gave us his most beautiful poem: *Plava Grobnica* (The Sea Grave). It is his greatest work of art and the most moving expression of an entire nation's sacrifice.

The survivors of the Serbian army and the refugees, once they crossed the ice and snow-covered mountains of Albania, reached the Greek islands of Corfu and Vido, known since then as the islands of death. These exhausted soldiers and refugees died in such large numbers that there was neither time nor space to bury the bodies. The corpses were loaded on boats and lowered into the sea, and the blue waves of the Mediterranean covered the place of their eternal rest. Most of them were without even a shroud.

Bojić's *Sea Grave* is almost inhuman. Its tone is one of cold desperation, for nothing warm or human could survive these tragic days. Far away the battles still raged, but here, where martyrs rested, a dead silence reigned.

Hold Imperial galleons! Stay your oars,
Proceed with calm,
In these holy waters, I say a proud mass
In midnight horror.

Beneath the sea, on sleeping shells
And weeds which gently fall,
Lies a grave of heroes, brother next to brother,
Prometheuses of hope, apostles of tragedy.

Don't you feel how gently the sea swells
Not to disturb their eternal rest?
. . . .
. . . .

And while the blue waves murmur over the entombed tragedy, in the distance, where the sun is stilll shining, the war continues, the same war for which these heroes died:

There, far away, the battlefields are flooded
With the same blood that is at rest here:
Here peace reigns over the fathers,
While sons there make history.

That's why I crave peace for this requiem,
Without words, tears, or weak sighs,
To unite the clouds of incense and gunpowder
With the muted rumbling of drums.

Hold Imperial galleons! In the name of respect
Glide without a sound.
I say a requiem like the heavens have yet to hear
Over these holy waters.

(Milutin Bojic, The Sea Grave)

Bojic was able to maintain the same high level of emotion through the entire poem. It is difficult, for the poem begins on a high peak, and a fall seems inevitable. The pathetic tone never rings false but, on the contrary, echoes with a ring of deep truth. The emotions are crystal clear and expressed logically in an excellent aesthetic form. All these qualities make this poem not only Bojic's best, but also a masterpiece of Serbian patriotic poetry.

Although some of Bojić's lyric poems may also be classified as epic poems, he wrote only two poems that definitely belong to the epic genre. One is *Kain*, published in Niš in 1915; the other is *Večna Sraža*, which he left unfinished and which was published as such in Corfu in the newpaper *Srpske Novine* on November 26 and December 1, 1916.

A vast epic vision is evident in his lyric poems *Pesme Bola i Ponosa*. His emotions are more actions than warm, human longings. Bojić was searching for a means of expression, as was Mestrović, who found his individual style after he abandoned the Viennese school and the influence of Rodin. Bojić, too, felt attracted to the majestic and grandiose–the powerful. This quality, which left Bojić's readers with the impression of looking at the world through a magnifying glass, led the poet frequently to use exaggerated expressions, which during the first phase of his poetry were often not in harmony with the emotions he presented. But with war and tragedy, the emotions grew to inhuman proportions and matched the powerful imagery. At that time, Bojić created such masterpieces as *Plava Grobnica* and *Petrovdanska Vizija*.

Logically, this should have led Bojić to give the best of himself in epic works. But artistic creativity is sometimes alien to reason and, unfortunately, his strictly epic poems are his weakest. Bojić seems bewildered by epic themes. The motifs of both his epic works are artisitically sound, but the poet seems to have lost himself in medieval imagery. Even more curious for this master of language and rhythm, his verse is imprecise and often lacks meaning. Poor choices of imagery and words are so flagrant that they often destroy the undoubted quality of some verses. This is true particularly of the poem *Kain*.

Kain was written in Niš, from May until August 1915, in three-verse stanzas. The first and third verses have nine syllables, and the second has eight in odd-numbered stanzas. In even-numbered stanzas, the method is reversed: 8-9-8. The verses rhyme according to the formula: aba, bcb, cdc, etc.; in other words, the second verse of each stanza rhymes with the first and third of the following one.

Kain has 558 verses, which are divided into three parts of different length. Part one contains 174 verses; part two, 294; and part three, 90.

Written during the anxious days of 1915, just before war broke out between Bulgaria and Serbia, the poem pictures Bulgaria joining with Austro-Hungary and Germany to destroy another Slav country; it is Cain murdering Abel. During a dark and tragic night, Cain rises from his eternal sleep and starts wandering through the world. The peace he sees around him tortures him. He meets Judas and asks him what is his quest. Judas answers that he is tortured by envy, for a new Judas has outdone him:

> His trumpets clarion infamy
> And treacherous is his horn,
> His knife is aimed at his brother.
>
> He betrayed his own God.
> His fame erases mine.
> Cain cried: "Show me him!"

And Judas leads Cain to show him this traitor, a traitor even greater than himself. He takes Cain through heaven on earth, through fields that once belonged to a peaceful and happy people. Finally, on the shores of the Rile (a river in Bulgaria), they meet Beelzebub:

> Cain then in his eyes poured
> The sap of black envy . . .

Beelzebub speaks of his desires and sings the praise of Cain: "Lead me, oh, my father!" Under Cain's guidance, Beelzebub attacks his brothers, the happy and peaceful people. Where flowed the peaceful Bregalnica (a river in Serbia) now flows blood. At the end of the struggle, justice triumphs, and the first part of the epic poem closes on this naive verse:

> The just remained pure and straight.

The second part of the poem is a succession of philosophical allegories. As mentioned already, Bojic was by no means a philosophical poet. His philosophy, especially when expressed through symbols and allegories, is at best naive, and this second part consists mostly of medieval allegories that make his ideas even more confusing. Cain succumbs to his conscience, and the Evil Spirit tells Cain about a girl who leads men into sin. Her name is *Desire*, and with her comes her brother *War*. Her bloodthirsty brother devastates towns, piles up dead bodies along his way, and leaves destruction and despair behind. But from all this destruction is born the *genius of Serbia*, and *good* triumphs over *evil*. However, victory is but temporary. The enemy crosses the river Drina between Serbia and Austro-Hungary. Blood is once again spilled, and peaceful villages disappear in flames. Cain renews his search for Beelzebub and finds him asleep on the shore of the Rile. He stirs in him again fury and envy, and death again rages in a country that had just found peace and justice.

In the third part, which contains only ninety verses, Bojić paints an image of a temporary peace, during which his people gather strength for new combats. Yet Cain continues to wander in search of evil.

These are the essential ideas and structure of the epic poem *Kain*. Bojić wanted to express, through symbols and allegories, the enormity of war between two Slavic countries. But he achieved only a maze of imagery, which confuses the reader and which sounds childishly naive. Several years later Bojić was to write beautiful poems of accepted sacrifice; *Kain*, however, abounds in shallow and pseudo-philosophical imagery. The symbols and allegories in *Kain* are grandiloquent, but they do not ring true, and their sheer numbers soon exhaust the reader.

The epic poem *Kain* does not come from a need to express deeply felt patriotic emotions. It is more a contemporary theme, which the poet had not experienced himself, but which he had taken from the historic context. It is also his first attempt to express the tragedy of war, but he had not yet known the deep anguish of exile nor witnessed the horror of genocide. The poet himself had not actually suffered, and the reader feels this clearly in the poems *Zemlja Oluje* and *Kain*. Later, when Bojic writes of the Albanian exodus, his poem has a sincerity that can result only from his personal participation in the tragedy of a nation.

Even his feeling for nature, which inspired beautiful imagery in his lyric poems, seems dead in *Kain*, and his descriptions seem to be more an exercise in verse-writing. This may easily be proved by comparing a description of nature in one of Bojić's first lyric poems with one in *Kain*, though in *Kain* the poet was no longer a novice.

When the floods of Danube shimmer with gold,
Burns the purple sky and smells the heat,
Scorching is the breath of meadows and paths
Huge burns the sun in its summer haze.
I feel the high noon in motionless time,
When the sun is large and reason silent,
Far away the trees in golden light,
Above them silently dies the time.

(M. Bojić, July Moon)

A description of nature in *Kain* is a mere cliché:

They hear the wings of eagles
And deep canyons call to them,
Attracted they are by cool forests.

Everywhere ferns. And oak trees,
The eternity of blue skies.
Laughing are rivers and meadows . . .

The lack of sincere emotion in the epic poem *Kain* led the poet to use a hackneyed imagery, which becomes even more tiring when he turns to philosophical allegory. For, when he was not deeply moved, Bojic reverted to the literary clichés of nineteenth-century poetry ("The cold breath of forests"—a phrase common in the previous century.)

The basic concept of Cain inspired Bojić, but because of its length and the poet's inexperience in this genre, the result was a poem which could not, and did not, survive as a good poem in Serbian poetry. Had the poet had time to polish and rework his poem, it might have been comparable to his dramatic and lyric works. However, *Kain* remains an unimportant attempt at epic writing with no great artistic value.

The epic poem *Večna Straža* (The Eternal Sentinel), was conceived and begun during the Albanian exodus and continued at Corfu. It is impossible to get a precise idea of what the poem would have been had it been completed, since we have only the small fragments that have been published. However, we do have a notion of what Bojić had wanted it to be. According to a manuscript note found in Bojić's papers,[1] *The Eternal Sentinel* was to consist of 1,500 verses on the theme of the tragic fate of the Serbian nation, a nation destined to be an eternal sentinel on the dangerous road that links the West with the Orient. According to another note in the same collection of Bojic's personal papers, he wanted this epic poem to have three parts: *Ecce gloria, Vanitas vanitatum,* and *Polio veru.* The published parts appeared in *Srpske Novine* at Corfu.[2] They are subtitled *Giljotina Sreće* (The Guillotine of Happiness) and labeled part IV, chapter II.

It appears that Bojić started with the fragments that touched his deepest feelings and that dealt with the recent days of the exodus. This part, *Giljotina Sreće* (The Guillotine of Happiness) is all that we have of the entire poem, and even after careful search of the poet's papers, no other fragment has ever appeared.

The Guillotine of Happiness comprises nine parts and 572 verses in all. The verses are of irregular length, and there is no stiff rhythmical pattern as in *Kain*. The poem itself is much more fluid than and not as tense as *Kain*. Though Bojić tried a genre that does not suit his talent, this published fragment of *Vecna Straza* contains verses that have the characteristic charm of Bojić's exalted romanticism.

---

[1] The manuscript note is presently in the possession of his nephew, Dragoslav Nikolić.

[2] *Srpske Novine*, godina 83, broj 100, November 26, 1916.

It is difficult to judge this fragment since we have no basis to evaluate the entire work. Most of these verses are far better than *Kain*, and the fragment as a whole is artistically superior, especially in the stanzas with Bojić's brilliant descriptions. This is his description of the Magician's death:

> The smell of burnt blood is like incense in Alhambra
> Like ripe roses, the pollen of lilies,
> Like musk, pomegranates, gold ember,
> Like roasted spices and mandragora's fumes.

The following passage given has a shorter rhythm, almost as if it were out of breath:

> She fights with screams. Her hair flies
> She is covered with blood, steeped in flowers.
> The executioner weaves a heavy net
> While passionate birds descend on her.

Nevertheless, there is no way to form a definite opinion about Bojić's epic poetry, for such an opinion would have to be based only on one youthful poem and a fragment of a later one. How much his talent would have developed must unfortunately remain an unanswered question. Personal sympathy and a liking for the poet are irrelevant; his epic poems definitely cannot compare with his lyric and dramatic works. They would not earn him the reputation of one of the best Serbian poets in the first decades of the twentieth century. His real artistic achievements, and they are undoubtedly great, lie in the fields of lyric and dramatic poetry.

In addition to his lyric and epic poems, Bojić also wrote drama in verse. An analysis of these works must take their lyric quality into account.

Bojić attempted to revive romantic and historic drama in verse, as Rostand had done in *L'Aiglon*. Even at the age of sixteen, he recognized the dramatic wealth in his country's past. However, it was not enough to sense the artistic possibilities in this past; he also had to acquire the dramatic skill and technique to treat these flamboyant themes correctly. A great deal of study and work was required before these historic and legendary events could be transposed into theatrical form.

Nineteenth-century authors who wrote of the Serbian past gave us flatly romantic plays. Their approach was enthusiastic indeed, but they produced anemic, bookish characters, who were mostly personifications of ideals or evils. They never seem to live forcefully on the stage. Thus, Bojić gets the credit for finding a new, though still romantic approach to the national past. He began studying records and not legends. He based his dramas upon carefully researched facts, and to do this, he read not only Serbian but foreign historians as well.

However, writing history was not his aim. He was trying to grasp the honest and true meaning of the past and to use this past for the re-creation of magnificent scenes. Bojić deeply admired Hugo and, like Hugo, tried to portray the grandeur of historic scenes against a sumptuous background. In this respect, the history of Serbia was a rich source for Bojić.

From early adolescence, Bojić was attracted to drama. It is taking a risk to guess what his future might have been, but in this case everything points to the conclusion that Bojić would have been a great Serbian dramatist had he not died at the age of twenty-five. Exalted sensuality belonged to the past; had he lived, the theme of pride and national suffering would have been assuaged by his return to a freed country, and historical dramas would probably have absorbed the greatest part of his creative energies.

Bojić was attracted to the drama because it was an art form suited to his artistic temperament since his early adolescence. For him theater was the brilliant vitality, the concentrated passion, the characters who lived and died for their passions amidst a sumptuous medieval setting.

Bojić was also interested in the theory of dramatic art. He was concerned with technical questions of dramatic composition, and he had a very personal and emotional point of view on the history of the Serbian drama. In an article on drama in Serbia, he gave his theory of the development of drama in Serbian literature.[3] The entire speech is based on brilliant imagery and is almost a textbook example of romantic prose writing.

It must be admitted that his brilliant metaphors outweigh his critical opinions. His concepts are clear, but, unfortunately, still superficial, often over-simplified, and intolerant. However, it must be noted, he was only eighteen.

Like typical romantic critics, Bojić judges a theater play by the impact it made on him and the like or dislike he felt for the author and his ideas. In this way, he ignores the importance of Joakim Vujić for the Serbian theater; as he states: "The contributions of Joakim Vujić are devoid of spontaneity or artistic importance. I believe the first writer of importance is Jovan Sterija Popović." This is a very personal statement, and a very enthusiastic one, but it can hardly be taken seriously. Bojić is not interested in the fact that the eighteenth-century theatrical legacy was—with the exception of the theater in Dubrovnik—only four translations of foreign plays. Joakim Vujić

[3] This speech was published later in the Viennese periodical *Zora* in 1911.

thus becomes the initiator of the original nineteenth-century theater in Serbia. Vujić also attracted and educated our first public. The notion that Sterija is the first playwright worth studying is youthful but naive.

Bojić berates the nineteenth-century writers because they did not understand the general spirit of the times they describe; in so doing, he commits the same error. Of all the playwrights of the nineteenth century, he considers only Jovan Sterija Popović and Laza Kostić worthwhile. He especially admires Kostić. Comedy does not exist in Serbian literature, according to Bojic, except in the works of Trifković, Glišić, and Nušić. In speaking of his contemporaries, Bojić quotes names that are now forgotten, such as Vojislav Jovanović, Svetislav Gredić, Dragoslav Nenadić, and Kosta Petrović. He does mention several excellent writers: Svetozar Ćorović, Ivo Ćipiko, and Aleksa Šantić.

Bojić's critical approach to historical tragedy as a literary genre in Serbian drama shows all the intolerance of youth. "One can say that all our writers of tragedies, be they good or bad, show the same weakness. They are filled with boring stereotypes, eternal idealizations of the characters, the inevitable patriotic tone, and the long Shakespearean monologue." It is difficult, even for an enthusiastic young man, to destroy the entire Serbian theatre of the nineteenth century with one blow.

The importance of the article lies in the fact that Bojić here presents a kind of literary credo. Anyone who seriously desires to understand the mechanism of Bojić's later dramatic works should read it. The personal concepts of the young poet, though poor literary criticism, are the basis on which he later built his plays. He is already aware that he does not want his characters to be idealized historical stereotypes. He wants them to labor under their own burdens and apply their personal will to the shaping of historical events. He strives to create living, human beings out of historical portraits. Yet the author must know and understand seemingly insignificant details of the historic period he is bringing back to life. This energetic rejection of history as but a colorful background is one of the great achievements of his otherwise highly romantic plays.

His next principle is: "Our drama must rely heavily on qualities and faults that are purely our own. In this way we can create characters that belong to our country and express our concerns." However, specific cultural qualities must be searched for and found in the physiology and psychology of the people, not in patriotic exaltation, and not in plays like J. Veselinović's *Djido* and S. Sremac's *Ivkova*

Slava, which are based mostly on patriotic folklore. If we take regional costume off Djido or the local accent away from Kalča only vague, imprecise, flat characters remain.

This principle was to be the basis of Bojić's fight against nineteenth century Serbian drama. He did not want to glorify the past through the creation of conventional and admirable characters. He wanted his historic characters to be real, or at least human beings the way he saw them. Because of this concept, he writes verses in the prologue of *Kraljeva Jesen* (The Autumn of a King) in which he begs his historical characters to forgive him for not indulging in the usual patriotic apotheosis:

> Forgive me, ghosts, and live again!
> In majestic garb pass by me,
> Singing days that will never return,
>
> We see that often you were small,
> But proud are we, for strong and brave,
> You did what you wanted and had to.
> We love you dearly—you're close to us!
> (M. Bojić, Prologue, The Autumn of a King)

These are the concepts which Bojić wanted to use when writing his historical dramas in verse; indeed, he did use them.

Because of the circumstances of Bojic's death, many of his manuscripts have been lost. Two of his dramas, *Lanci* and *Gospodja Olga*, were definitely lost in the upheaval of war and exile. Other manuscripts were in the possession of people who either did not recognize their value or did not feel that they should be published.

At the age of sixteen, Bojić planned to write a trilogy of dramas in verse, under the title of *Despotova Kruna* (The Crown of the Despot). It was to consist of three separate dramas, use the same characters, and have a continuous plot line from one drama to the next.

The manuscript of the first drama is presently in the National Library in Belgrade. The widow of Professor Nikola Mirković sold it to the National Library in 1943. The manuscript consists of twelve sheets of paper, with writing on both sides. For many years, it was thought lost, until it was discovered by Dr. Miraš Kićović, who communicated the news of his discovery to the Serbian Academy of Science.

The drama is without a title, or at least it appears to be, since the title may have been on a separate page, now lost. On the first page of this manuscript, Bojić briefly describes the characters and proceeds immediately with the verses of the play. At the end it is signed "Bojić," and it is dated December 20-30, 1907.

The inspiration for the drama seems to come from the Tower of Vršac, the last rampart that the Despot Djurdje Branković wanted to hold out against the Turkish invasion. In 1907, Bojić spent his summer vacation in Bečkerek at the home of his mother's sister Anne, the wife of Dušan Cvejanović. While there, he saw the Tower of Vršac. The tower and its romantic past must have deeply impressed the young man, since it seems to have inspired this untitled drama.

Miraš Kićović believes that this drama is the first part of the dramatic trilogy *Despotova Kruna*. His opinion is well-founded, for this drama belongs chronologically to the period preceding *Slepi Despot* and to that of a third drama, which also has no title. The manuscripts of the two other dramas from Bojić's early youth are presently among Bojić's papers owned by his nephew, Dragoslav Nikolić. Kićović also supports his opinion by referring to Bojić's handwritten note, in which the poet mentions a drama in verse: *Despot Lazar*. In the drama Kićović discovered, Despot Lazar is the central character.

This manuscript is the work of a novice, in the full meaning of the word. But there are few novices capable of writing some of the verses scattered throughout this drama. It should also be noted that this drama contains the germs of all the future qualities the poet was to develop.

The second manuscript, owned by Dragoslav Nikolić, bears the title *Despotova Kruna–trologija* and the subtitle *Slepi Despot–dramska poema u jednom činu*. This is the same drama that Bojić's friend, Radoslav Vesnić, took to Rista Odavić in the National Theater in 1908. Later, when he had become a successful poet, Bojić recognized the shortcomings of this early work and refused to have it published. On the manuscript is written, in the poet's own handwriting, "Today, February 11, 1911, I understood that this drama is without value." Signed: "Bojić." Then follows a remark that the drama was written in 1908 and copied in 1909.

The third part of this trilogy occurs in two versions of the same drama, both without title. There is no mention of this third part in any of Bojić's papers, and we therefore have no indication of what its title may have been. The manuscripts are in Nikolić's collection of papers, and the characters are the same as in the two preceding works.

The three dramas of this trilogy were written by a high school student and are obviously the works of a beginner. They are of interest for the study of later works, such as *Kraljeva Jesen* and *Uroševa Ženidba*, but they are otherwise without intrinsic artistic value.

Bojić's collected papers also contain fragments of the first two acts of a drama entitled *Vejavica* (Snowstorm). According to Bojić's friend Vesnić, the poet intended to make it a drama in four acts, but the fragments belong to two different versions of this project. One of the manuscripts carried the seal of the hospital in Thessaloniki and the notation Dj. 12, which proves that Bojić carried this manuscript through Albania and kept it with him until his death. Unfortunately, these fragments are far too brief to warrant even a superficial judgment of the poet's intentions.

Thus, Bojić's contribution to the Serbian drama consists of two published mature works—*Kraljeva Jesen* and *Uroševa Ženidba*—and the manuscripts of his early works. According to Dragoslav Nikolić, the manuscripts of *Gospodja Olga* and *Lanci* were lost in Thessaloniki after the poet's death.

The two published dramas are the work of a poet who has matured through war and suffering. They do not merely show the potentialities of a talented young man; they are two great achievements in the history of Serbian drama.

Kraljeva Jesen (The Autumn of a King), a drama in Alexandrine verse consisting of one act with a prologue, was written in 1912.

Bojić carefully went into great detail for each of his characters, even to the point of giving their ages: King Milutin, 60; Konstantin, the King's son by his first wife, 38; Simonida, the King's fourth wife, 23; Theodora Smiljac, the wife of Stephan, the King's son by his third wife, 24; Dušan, 7; Danilo, the Father Superior of the convent of Hilendar, 42; the Duke Novak Grebostrek, 50; Constanza Morozini, wife of King Vladislav's nephew, 37; Dimitrije Paleologue, brother of Simonida, the King's fourth wife; Guillaume Adam, Archbishop of Bar and French historian; two Franciscan monks, pages, court ladies, noblemen servants with torches. The action takes place in the King's palace in Pauni in 1314.

The action is simple and leads straight into the important dialogue between Simonida and Danilo. Simonida, daughter of the Byzantine Emperor, Andronikus II, became the fourth wife of the Serbian King Milutin through an intricate play of political influences. When the drama opens, she is 23 years old and at the peak of her youth and beauty. In contrast, the King is in his declining years; his grandchildren are warriors, the same age as Simonida. Still dreaming of the court of Byzantium as a lost paradise and remembering vividly its sumptuous magnificence, Simonida feels as if she were a total stranger at the Serbian court. She does not love the old King, her husband. She is beautiful, vulnerable, and predestined for love. In such an atmosphere, many hearts at court burn with passion for her, but these torches throw light only on the path that leads to her cold nuptial chambers, until finally she surrenders to the same love Phaedra has known: she falls in love with her stepson Stephan. But Bojić does not touch on the ethics of her love and does not raise the moral issue of incest. Simonida does not think her love is a sin, while Phaedra dies because of it. All that Simonida wants is the fulfillment of her passionate love. She wants happiness, and her desire is accentuated by the dark shadow of the cage in which her luxuriant youth is trapped. To get Stephan, she is ready to pay any price.

The characters are described simply but forcefully. "Coming up the court staircase is Danilo. His face is energetic and virile. The hair and beard are black. The features are powerful and clean cut." The description of King Milutin is equally concise. "The King is sixty years old. Tall, strongly built, well preserved, though his face shows signs of a life filled with war and passions. His eyes are blurred, but still alive and reflect the fire that once burned in them. His clothes glitter, and his husky voice lends a mysterious poetic tone to this personification of vanity, handsomeness, and passion, through the ashes of which one can sense only jealousy." Apart from the elaborate notes on her clothing, the description of Simonida is even shorter. "She is a twenty-three year old woman who possesses all the qualities required to make men happy through love, but her marital tragedy has marked her still childish features with all the suffering of unfulfilled desires and has given them the attraction, irresistibly sad, of a premature maturity."

The entire drama rests on the conflict among these three characters. Danilo persuades the King to have his son Stephan blinded for his attempted rebellion and thus to set a terrible example for anyone tempted to disrupt the peace of the kingdom. Simonida loves Stephan and fights to save him. She goes to Danilo, knowing, as a woman, that if she pleaded with the King, she would only awaken his jealousy and make him more adamant. She hopes to use the all-powerful Danilo to achieve her aim. However, Danilo rejects her plea and uses his influence to strengthen the King in his decision. A herald is sent to Skoplje, and Stephan will be blinded.

Kraljeva Jesen is a lyrical drama in one act. Therefore, it focuses on a single psychological confrontation—that of Simonida and Danilo in the crucial scene of the play.

There are relatively few critiques of this play, and, even more interesting, not one presents the drama in its proper light. No literary critic has placed the dramatic accent on the scene between

Simonida and Danilo, which is, in my opinion, the essential scene of the drama. Nor have the critics seen Danilo and Simonida as the main protagonists. The jealousy of the aging King is not the crux of the drama. It is rather the conflict between two concepts of life, two distinct emotional attitudes—Simonida versus Danilo and greed for happiness versus greed for power.

In most cases, the leading women in lyrical dramas are not sensual; rather, they are "Madonnas" as in Maeterlinck's Aglaene and Beatrice, or as in the heroines of Gerhardt Hauptman's lyric dramas. Sometimes they reach the high summits of romanticism, as does Elizabeth in *Tannhauser* or Krimhilde in *Gotterdammerung*. But Simonida is nothing more and nothing less than a young woman who wants to live. She does not strive to be as strong as Hedda Gabler, but is not as resigned as Nora or even Beata. Free of complexes and bursting with vitality, she craves only for a ray of sunshine in the darkness around her. Her whole tragedy is contained in her scream: "Light! Give me light!" She sees herself clearly and describes her emotions in answer to Danilo's summons:

> Oh, you sacrifice happiness for eternity;
> I will not give lilies for a crown of thorns!
> Eternity I don't wish—I am just a woman!

As a woman, for Bojić, she wants only the happiness of the present moment. This is her strength and her weakness as well. She knows that her strength has its roots in her weakness, and in fighting Danilo she will use her feminity as her strongest asset.

The critics who have studied *Kraljeva Jesen* (Krsto Ljumović and Petar Taletov) think that Simonida accepts her fate too readily. According to Ljumović: "King Milutin accepts that his son Stephan, whom Simonida loves, is blinded; Danilo, though he dreams about Simonida's beauty, does not fight to conquer her; and Simonida abandons herself to her fate in an almost childish way."[4] Taletov repeats the same: "The King easily accepts that his son is blinded; Simonida offers her body to Danilo with great ease and accepts her fate without difficulty; Danilo gives up all the sensual dreams he lived in his monk's cell without too much effort."[5] These two literary critics are under the impression that the essential problem of this lyrical drama was resolved too simply.

---

[4] Krsto Ljumović, "Štampane Drame M. Bojića," *Zapisi*, Knjiga I (1927).

[5] Petar Taletov, "Kraljeva Jesen, Drama u Jednom Činu M. Bojića," *Delo*, Knjiga 49 (1913).

The only person who easily abdicated his will, in my opinion, is King Milutin. The drama would be greatly flawed if Milutin and Simonida were indeed the main protagonists, as these two critics think. But if Danilo, and not Milutin, is the lead, then there is no such "flaw." Milutin becomes, thus, of secondary importance. He is still constructed logically, but his psyche does not require any subtle or detailed analysis.

Simonida and Danilo by no means surrendered meekly to their fate. In the first place, Danilo shows no traces of having surrendered his will power. He is not an oriental fatalist and, as for all artistically valid protagonists in drama, his fate is the result of a struggle within himself. If he sacrifices his desire for Simonida to his ambition, it is because he has willed it so.

Furthermore, his sacrifice lies not only in the rejection of his sensual dreams, as Ljumović and Taletov think; it is infinitely greater: the personal happiness of a peaceful life. All this he does to achieve one goal: the fulfillment of his ambition. However, Danilo's ambition is not that of a petty courtier, for he could have power through Simonida by saving Stephan. Rather, his ambition is that of a statesman and leader, and his goal is the grandeur of the state. It is hard to understand why critics failed to ntoice this distinction, since generations of young readers have fully appreciated the nobility and spirit of dedication expressed in Danilo's monologue.

This dramatic conflict is the key to the lyrical drama *Kraljeva Jesen*. The dramatic decision Danilo must make is the psychological resolution of the action, and it is indeed strange that Bojić's critics have failed to understand this. Danilo succumbs to his own strength in the same way in which Simonida falls prey to her own weakness. Thus, both protagonists proceed directly to the sacrifice of their own happiness.

It is strange that Bojić, who was essentially a romantic in the style of Victor Hugo, did not base the action of his drama on exterior forces, but followed the principle of neo-classical tragedy, in which the action is a logical result of the psychological forces that create the inner crisis and consequently resolve it. Each of the main protagonists carries in himself or herself all the elements of his or her personal tragedy. But Bojić's protagonists are not true neo-classical heroes. Unfortunately, they are static. They are at the end what they are at the beginning. They do not change in the course of their conflicts and sufferings, and because of this psychological rigidity, they sometimes seem almost inhuman. From the very beginning, Bojić constructed his protagonists in a logical and final way, which deprives them of the fluidity of real life. They only shape the dramatic action, but are not formed by it. Thus, they seem to live outside of the action, as if psychologically petrified even before the action starts. They are lyrical portraits rather than dramatic protagonists, and they are far too simplified to personify emotions.

Bojić showed great respect for the historically accurate detail, but he created dramatic characters in a way that corresponded to his personal lyrical concepts. In this he was a pure romantic.

It is more than probable that, compared to the magnificence of Byzantium, the Serbian court at Pauni seemed somber and austere to Simonida. We also know that Simonida's brothers, returning from a visit they paid her at the Serbian court, described it in unflattering and bitter words. Yet the love Simonida feels for her stepson Stephan is Bojic's invention. Grigorije Camblak, the official historiographer of King Milutin's court, goes so far as to say that Milutin had Stephan blinded because Simonida wanted him blinded. Among modern historians, Zečević considers Camblak incorrect, but Stojan Novaković and Ljuba Kovačević regard it as a serious possibility. Nor was the relationship between Milutin and Simonida really as it was in Bojić's drama. Mihailo Laskaris, in his book *The Byzantine Princesses*, maintains that Simonida returned to Byzantium after the death of Milutin. When Milutin was proclaimed a saint by the Orthodox church, Simonida sent to Serbia "a gold church candelabra of great value and other gifts." If her life with Milutin was not a great romantic love, neither was it the dramatic version Bojić created.

As a poet, Bojić took the liberty of presenting history to fit his lyrical talent, as Corneille did in *The Cid* and Schiller did in *Don Carlos*. Milutin, Simonida, and Danilo were the three forces Bojić used to build a drama—his lyrical vision of an historical situation.

Kraljeva Jesen is above all a lyrical drama, as Bojić was above all a lyric poet. The entire drama is bathed with intense emotionality. Though it does rely on psychological study, Bojić must have felt a deep relief whenever he could free himself from inner motivations and abandon himself to exalted emotions. At moments it is as if he were rushing over unavoidable obstacles in order to reach scenes of emotional confrontation. From the moment he brought Simonida and Danilo face to face, Bojić lost the patience to develop this key scene gradually and lead us through a careful progression of theatrical effects. Bojić seemingly hurries to arrive at the clash of exalted emotions and, thus, gives to the critics the opportunity to reproach him for his lack of psychological verisimilitude.

The magnificence of the medieval settings had a strong appeal for the romantic poet. For Bojić, the appeal of the Middle Ages is not condensed in one perfect detail that stands for an entire bygone civilization, as in Hérédia's *Le Vitrail*. It is rather the opulent atmosphere of medieval courts, with an intensity of flamboyant color. In his verses, Bojić brings the flamboyant and oriental luxury of the medieval Serbian court back to life. The poet has a deep affinity for the barbaric splendor of these days:

> Where green marble, and agate, and opal
> Shimmer, and shines the golden fresco
> Of court receptions . . . Proud palatines
> With silver helmets near the huge gate,
> Guards with tunics with glittering rubies,
> The whole court veiled in purple brocade.
> On the floor carpets of Persian origin,
> Covered with roses and pomegranate blossoms.
> The throne in sunlight, while two golden lions
> Sleep at the feet of the most powerful emperor
> Behind the throne a cross of gold and coral,
> And a sycamore filled with golden birds
>
> The barbarian envoys of Rome and Ragusa,
> Venice, Paris . . . from all that dust
> Of lizards crawling at the Pope's feet
> Feels faint in front of that splendor . . . [6]

The visual impact of Byzantine splendor seduces Bojić. Skerlić's influence pushed him in this direction, as the critic felt that the magnificent power and refinement of Byzantium was bound to bolster the national pride of the Serbs.

But Bojić was a romantic of the twentieth century. He looked through historical documents to find accurate details for his descriptions of medieval courts. For *Kraljeva Jesen*, his bibliography included: Florinski, *Byzance aux deuxième quart du XI-ème siècle, tome 2*; Brocart, *Indication pour un voyage en Terre Sainte*; Jireček, *Histoire du peuple serbe*; Gelzer, *Bizantinische Kulturgeschichte*; Charles Diehl, *Byzantine Art*; and the writings of the Archbishop Danilo. Bojić approached the study of the medieval past seriously, and only then attempted to transpose it into lyrical romantic drama.

Kraljeva Jesen opened on October 19, 1913, in the National Theater in Belgrade. The composer Miloje Milojević wrote the musical

---

[6] When Bojić wrote these verses, Rokpros had done a well-known and much-appreciated painting, depicting a barbaric envoy completely dazed by the splendor of a reception at the Byzantine court.

overture entitled *The Symphonic Prologue to Simonida*. The production met with only partial success. There were two reasons for this: first, the drama lacked theatrical effects and is much less powerful on stage than when read; second, the actors of the time were not capable of projecting the metallic beauty of Bojić's verse. The leading actress, Taborska, lacked the temperament and inner fire to communicate the consuming passion of Simonida, and her lukewarm performance robbed the entire drama of its meaning. She was a conscientious actress, but the romantic role of Simonida required fire and inspiration rather than meticulous work. Ljuba Stanojević, as Danilo, was stiff and artificial and gave the impression that he was trying to recapture the successes of his previous career rather than create a vital and powerful Danilo. Gavrilović, as King Milutin, was cold and uninspired. The other actors were simply deplorable, according to the press reviews of the time, and managed to quench the passionate fire of the play. Thus, poor acting deprived *Kraljeva Jesen* of the success it deserved, and not until twenty years later did the play achieve the success it so greatly merited.

Bojić began another drama in verse, *Uroševa Ženidba*, in Niš in 1915, and finished it in Corfu in 1916. The first version had four acts, but the poet later condensed it into three acts. The manuscript of the four-act version has been lost.[7] At this time, the poet became completely involved in the writing of *Pesme Bola i Ponosa*, and he died before he had time to polish *Uroševa Ženidba* for publication. The drama was published four years after his death *(Srpski Književni Glasnik, Nova Serija*, Knjiga II, 1921), and presented for the first time two years later in the National Theater in Belgrade.

The characters in the drama are the Emperor; the Empress; King Uroš, the Emperor's son; Siniša Nemanjić, the Emperor's half-brother; Tomanda, daughter of Anna Paleologue; a distant relative of the Emperor, the captain Palmar, and others. In this play, Bojić did not precisely set the time and place of the action as he did in *Kraljeva Jesen*. All we know is that the action takes place at the court of the Emperor Dušan at a time near the end of his reign.

The dramatic construction is more elaborate than in his preceding drama. It contains fewer lyrical elements and more dramatic qualities. The entire action relies on the dramatic contrast between the personalities of the Emperor Dušan, known in Serbian tradition as "Dušan the Powerful," and his son "Uroš the Weak." The Emperor is condemned to leave his empire to this weak son. Dušan has built an

---

7 According to Miss Todorovic, Bojic's fiancee.

empire using all his strength and energy, an empire that is his whole life's work. He recognizes the weakness of his son and seeks to establish an alliance, through his son's marriage, with a powerful foreign nation. Looking even farther into the future, the Emperor hopes for a grandson who might be a monarch worthy of the empire. But Uroš is in love, and his dreams are of happiness and not of war. He loves Tomanda, the daughter of Anna Paleologue, a poor relative who lives at his father's court. Tomanda is a beautiful young girl, bursting with vitality. The dreamy weakness of Uroš does not appeal to her. She loves Siniša, the Emperor's half-brother. Siniša is strong and brave. Unlike Uroš, Siniša does not implore Tomanda for her love—he makes her love him.

Dušan cannot find a foreign princess worthy of his heir, and he agrees to let Uroš marry Tomanda. Under pressure from this powerful Emperor, who does not hesitate to threaten her with death at the stake, Tomanda gives her consent. However, she elopes with Siniša, and all Uroš's dreams are shattered. The Empress persuades Dušan not to pursue the fugitives, since Tomanda is no longer worthy of the throne. The Emperor abandons himself to his dreams of conquest, and, at the moment when he has a vision of the entire world at his feet, he sees the weak Uroš standing in front of him. His dream dies, as does Uroš's dream of happiness. The Emperor is left alone with the tragic vision of the collapse of his Empire after his death.

The action in *Uroševa Ženidba* follows a logical course. The drama rests on the inevitable clash between two diametrically opposed personalities: the Emperor and his son. The Emperor is above all a man of action who looks at other men and at events with a clear, precise practicality. Like all men who have achieved great success through their own energy, Dušan is not bothered by scruples. But his own son, Uros, will remain to the end of the play an enigma. Dušan cannot understand a weakness that resolves problems in drinking bouts or melancholic tears. His morals are those of a conqueror, not of a monk. Uroš's unhappiness is, unfortunately, low-keyed and too personal to be a serious counterpart to Dušan's tragedy. Thus, Bojić has presented a one-sided conflict, since the son is no antagonist to the father, and the play is sadly out of balance.

The character of Siniša is not sufficiently developed. When Bojić started writing *Uroševa Ženidba*, Siniša seemed to be a means of expressing the poet's own views on life. Siniša is strangely reminiscent of the poet his friends described before the wars. "Siniša is handsome and tall. He represents a type of passionate and elegant Greek . . . The slight irony of his smile and the shrewdness hidden in the corners of his eyes are baffling, and people never know if he is speaking seriously or only joking. There is always a mockery in his tone."

Like the young Bojić, Siniša is a man who speaks passionately of love and sensually of a kiss. The poet began by expressing through Siniša his own passionate and enthusiastic youth, but under the impact of war and exile, he abandoned this theme and began to stress the tragic conflict between the Emperor and his son. Thus, Siniša is left behind, just as Bojić had left his own careless youth behind.

The entire drama rests on the protraits of the Emperor and his son Uroš. The strength of the conflict reaches its peak in the last scene and is contained in the silent opposition of these two portraits. The other characters are mainly used to give depth to these two figures.

Regardless of certain shortcomings, in comparison with *Kraljeva Jesen, Uroševa Ženidba* represents a great evolution of Bojić's dramatic talent. It is a complete drama in three acts. The lyrical elements are better controlled, and the dramatic construction is more mature. The transitions between scenes are smoother, while the lyrical scenes are better motivated psychologically. On the other hand, *Kraljeva Jesen* has such a lyrical intensity that it moves the reader more deeply and rings more young and true. The irreproachable verses of *Uroševa Ženidba* as well as its brilliant scenes do not have the exaltation of youth and the bewitching charm of *Kraljeva Jesen*.

In *Uroševa Ženidba* Bojić applied the same aesthetic principles as in *Kraljeva Jesen*. He avoids the idealized and stereotyped historic figures and situations that were so dear to the writers of the nineteenth century. He tries to give his protagonists some psychological motivation for their actions and to make them living human beings, with human errors and virtues. It is no accident that Bojić did not portray the Emperor Dušan at his coronation, at the peak of his power, but in a moment of doubt and suffering. This is a very unusual approach to the mythical figure of "Dušan the Powerful" in Serbian history.

As far as his treatment of Uroš is concerned, had Bojić taken the nineteenth-century approach, he would have drawn from the wealth of Serbian folklore the poems and legends that deal with Uroš the Weak. But he tried to avoid the dramatic concepts of Emanuel Kozacinski's *Uroš V* and the later adaptation by Jovan Rajić.

The first presentation of *Uroševa Ženidba* was in the National Theater in Belgrade in 1923. This play was slightly more successful than *Kraljeva Jesen* had been in 1913. The management of the theater had gone to great pains to ensure a correct and even lavish evocation of the medieval atmosphere. Brailovski had designed splendid costumes, for which he found inspiration in medieval frescoes. However, the actors' delivery of the verses was flat and failed to move the audience. The lyrical intensity of the conflict and the pathos of the last scene were lost. Ginić as the Emperor, and Gnjatić as the Empress were weak, and M.M. Bogić, Nikolić, and Milošević were simply inadequate.

Bojić, with his talent, his lyricism, and his sense of the stage, would have brought a rebirth to national romantic drama had he not died so young. He was the first Serbian poet who tried to create a truly historical atmosphere for romantic drama in verse and to delineate characters who were real people, who were bursting with an inner vitality. These two published dramas are the creations of a strong and poetic artist and bring to Serbian poetry verses of extreme beauty.

INFLUENCES IN SERBIAN POETRY

There are two important foreign influences on the poetry of Milutin Bojić: Charles Baudelaire and Oscar Wilde. These influences never blend together into a single style. Rather, they run through Bojić's poems and dramas in separate channels, as it were, and it is easy to follow their course at any given time.

Bojić had too much vitality and youthful sensuality to appreciate fully the refinements of perverse voluptuousness. His vigorous temperament did not need the crutch of a perverse imagination, and, had he not fallen under Baudelaire's influence, his youthful poems would sound much more sincere. In spontaneous moments in his early poems, Bojić's sensuality was simply the result of his young and rich blood; it was not, as in Baudelaire, a way to annihilate the suffering of thought. This is the difference between their two sensualities: Bojić's was an aim unto itself, Baudelaire's was an anesthetic.

But Baudelaire's sensuality contains an element that the critic Skerlić did not notice. If the romantic poet Alfred de Musset asserted that sensuality is the death of soul love, Baudelaire involuntarily proved that sensuality ultimately kills voluptuousness itself. In reading Baudelaire, we can understand the desperate suicide of the jaded man, who reaches a state in which he is so saturated with physical sensations that he is totally unable to experience any new sensations. When voluptuousness can no longer intoxicate the senses, Baudelaire will face the tragedy of utter meaninglessness. Sensuality is thus an anesthetic that deadens every nerve of the French poet, and he has to use physical pain to bring his numbed senses back to life again.

Baudelaire has all the marks of a "decadent poet:" a refined scepticism, a morbid exaltation of the senses, and an utter inability to reach a union between mystical aspirations and a higher ideal. But Bojić's poetry bears none of these marks. Baudelaire worshipped spleen, Bojić his own vitality. Baudelaire would deplore the destruction of the over-civilized Athens, while Bojić would sing the triumph of the Macedonian.

In his refinement, Baudelaire is subject to all the nuances. Perfumes exalt him more than tangible realities. On the contrary, Bojić revels in tangible realities, which he expresses in words that definitely lack nuances: "I bite," "I drink passion" (*"grizem," "pijem strasti"*). His sensuality is direct; all he wants is to grasp life with both hands and drink.

Delights, delights, delights, deep, endless!
M. Bojić, Hymn to Life

But in his desire to emulate Baudelaire's *Flowers of Evil*, Bojić felt that no sensation was strong enough to introduce an unconventional sensuality into Serbian poetry. The contrast he wanted to achieve can easily be understood by comparing his description of a kiss and that of Milosav Jelić:

And tell you the song of sun itself,
When to part our lips means to die.
(M. Bojić, Sonnet XXXII)

Embrace me with your arm, white and pink as a rose,
And dissolve, my soul, in an eternal kiss.
(M. Jelić, Passion)

Thus, Bojić tried to avoid the conventional passion found in the Serbian poetry of his time by using the audacity of Baudelaire's poetic vocabulary. All the "livid sweat" and "morbid blood" in Bojić's poetry comes from Baudelaire's influence. When Bojić is himself, sincere and spontaneous, he gives us poems of brutal vitality, as in *David in Love, Salome, The Song of David*. But when he tries to emulate Baudelaire, he sounds affected, and such youthful poems as *The Ghost* and *Griphos* lack sincerity.

The poem *Avet* (The Ghost) even has a French subtitle: *Joie de Vivre*. The first stanza is pure Bojić,

I want to drink the dreamy eyes of women
And bite their lips, playing with them,
Watch the lilies as they slowly wilt
While I waste my youth in wine and smoke.

Then follows an exalted dream, which clearly owes much to Baudelaire,

Yes, yes, I'll roar with laughter, drunk with fury,
In the sweet embrace of fallen virtue,
Drinking the breath of women of flesh and blood,
Breathing in the passion of their breasts.
(M. Bojić, The Ghost)

From then on, the poem becomes a reflection of the *Flowers of Evil*.

In *Griphos*, the atmosphere clearly belongs to Baudelaire,

Deep into me you dug your nails,
And in a scream I tear at my own breast,
I bite my own flesh and moan, while
I feel you break my virile ribs. . .
(M. Bojić, Griphos)

The poet of *Flowers of Evil* could well have signed these verses.

Baudelaire inspired many stanzas in Bojić's youthful poetry. In them Bojić goes beyond the bounds of normal voluptuousness and, under Baudelaire's influence, enters the domain of sadism.

> I want to cut my veins in that moment
> For you to put your thirsty lips on them
> And drink my blood, while your desires fade
> And while I die have you warm my body.
>
> Then poisoned by the smell of my corpse,
> I want you to bite me as my limbs go rigid,
> I want you to scream with bile in your blood,
> And to know consciously the haughty pride
> Of the wild, insane love, when it is blood that loves.
>
> (M. Bojić, Whipped by the Wind)

This is, without doubt, the atmosphere of *Flowers of Evil*. "Blood" dominates, not the young, healthy blood of Bojić's other youthful poems, but Baudelaire's poisoned blood.

When such "poisoned passion" does not pretend to be a sincere expression of the young poet's emotions, but evokes an atmosphere of exalted voluptuousness, either historical or legendary, it can achieve high artistry, precisely through its exaggeration. Bojić sang the Biblical David, his sensuality that "made lips purple and livid" (*čini usne modre i zelene*). Not only is the artistic level high, but it also represents an entirely new theme in Serbian poetry of the twentieth century

In his *David*, Bojić understood and expressed perfectly the essential characteristic of perversion: the constant dulling of the threshhold of nervous sensitivity, which leads to a need for ever stronger stimuli that conventional sensations no longer provide. This is quite clear in Baudelaire's poetry at a spontaneous level, but Bojić made it a conscious explanation of David's perverse sensuality:

> Time erased colors from my parched lips,
> My heart is wax, my breast infected,
> My dried tongue is glued to my wilted throat.
>
> . . . .
>
> . . . .
>
> I want my youth with its golden fringe,
> Waves of your blood to moisten my wounds,
> To bring back the roar of youthful days
> When I sang for Saul hymns that made insane,
> When I knew the bond of Mykha's lips.
>
> (M. Bojić, David in Love)

When Bojić's exaltation is not spontaneous and sincere, he remembers Baudelaire and wilfully attempts to reach the level he desires.

For this reason, in most cases, Baudelaire's influence on Bojić is unfortunate. It is more a crutch Bojić used in the absence of spontaneous emotions than it is the channeling of sincere emotions into new aesthetic forms. Even in his youth, Bojić is really not a "cursed poet." He is only an adolescent poet whose first poems expressed an unusual temperament with unusual sincerity.

Bojić was also strongly influenced by Oscar Wilde, specifically by *Salome*.

At the beginning of the twentieth century, the works of Oscar Wilde, *De Profundis* and *The Portrait of Dorian Gray*, were published in Serbia. This was followed by the performance of Wilde's *Salome* in Belgrade's National Theater. The play met with tremendous success since *Salome*, the beauty of whose lyrical elements make it more poetry than drama, was in complete harmony with the artistic tendencies of the new wave of Serbian poets.

The influence of Wilde's *Salome* on Bojić was immediate and extremely strong. It is evident not only in Bojić's poem *Salome* and all his later poems with Biblical themes, but also in the concept and form of his later lyrical dramas.

The same quality of exalted sensuality overflows from Wilde's *Salome* into Bojić's *Salome* and from there into Bojić's other Biblical poems. When Bojić's Mary Magdalene mourns for Christ, it is not mourning in the spirit of the Gospel. She does not mourn the death of a spiritual Christ, but the death of a man she loved. Her love is exalted and entirely Wildean. Her desire for Him still lives, as does the desire of Salome for Johanan. Mary Magdalene cries at the foot of the cross,

> How beautiful you are! Even dead, I want you!

This cry is directly influenced by Wilde's *Salome* and is a repetition of the kiss she gives, in Wilde's play, to the dead lips of Johanan. Bojić's Mary Magdalene is a direct heir of Wilde's *Salome*.

The difference lies only in the moment at which the two poets choose to represent Salome. Wilde painted Salome in her initial exaltation for Johanan, but Bojić, with a cruel logic, showed her embittered and painful death, at a time when her body was nothing more but wounded and decomposing flesh. But the poetic inspiration comes from the same source, as Bojić's *Salome* grew out of Wilde's interpretation of the Biblical theme.

The Salome of both Wilde and Bojić is driven by her violent blood. This is true of all the Biblical characters whom Bojić depicts later. On one hand, the body is overwhelmed by blood thick and morbid with voluptuousness (Salome, Herodiade, Herod); on the other, this same body is destroyed without mercy, for the body is nothing compared to the soul (Johanan). These poems are examples of total dissociation of body and soul, one of the basic concepts in many works of Western literature. It lies at the root of Baudelaire's mystical Satanism and obsession with sin. Aldous Huxley's *Spendrell* is a curious repetition of this dissociation of soul and body as well as an illustration of Baudelaire's relationship with his step-father, General Aupick. In Wilde, this total separation into antagonistic body and soul leads to a twofold perversity—the sensual and the ethical.

After the *Portrait of Dorian Gray* appeared, Wilde was attacked by English critics, for he had completely denied the basic English morality of the time. The immediate success of Wilde's works in Serbia had nothing to do with his ethics, or, for that matter, with his morbidity. The new Serbian poets were simply awed by the brilliancy of form, the virtuosity of imagery. Certain poets, among them Bojić, were thrilled by the beauty of Wilde's descriptions, which literally shimmered with rich adjectives.

Bojić's healthy youth prevented him from accepting the credo of "decadent" poets. From Wilde he took what he had already taken from Baudelaire: a search for extremes that transgress humanly possible reactions and impulses.

> I wandered through filthy harbors
> Searching for passion in muddy boats,
> At morning watchmen found me drunk
> And whipped my back and shoulders.
> —Women drank my passion to the very bones!
> I screamed in tents of warriors,
> While pain set on my eyes, lips, and breasts,
> Happy when I tortured, as well as when tortured. . .
>
> (M. Bojić, Salome)

Wilde's Salome, the woman who holds the severed head of Johanan in her blood-stained hands, is the image of an atrocious power, the destructive power of a desire that nothing can quench. "What can I do now, Johanan?" is Salome's tragic question, while her eyes are glued to the dead lips of the prophet, "Neither rivers, nor all the waters of the sky can extinguish my passion." The cruelty in Wilde's drama is not the death of Johanan, but the useless kiss that Salome imprints on his ice-cold lips.

The Biblical rhythm and accentuation—even the archaic form "thou art"—is another important feature of Wilde's influence on Bojić. The most important discovery for Bojic was Wilde's use of Biblical language and rhythm to express majestic simplicity. Images seem to fall spontaneously into stanzas, and their vastness permeates the entire poem. In all his works, Wilde uses frequently the sober and majestic Biblical structure. The same is true of Bojić, but his Biblical style owes more to the influence of Wilde than to the Bible itself.

Wilde's *Salome* influenced not only Bojić's lyrical poems, but his lyric dramas as well, primarily *Kraljeva Jesen* (The Autumn of a King). All the protagonists live exclusively for the fulfillment of their desires. Wilde's Salome thinks only of Johanan, the young Syrian captain only of Salome, Herodiade of her vengeance, and Herod of death. In the same way Simonida is overwhelmed by her love for Stephan, Danilo by his lust for power, and the King by his jealousy. All the protagonists are driven by one and only one force. In this way, both Wilde and Bojić restricted the psychological make-up of their characters, but thereby gained lyrical intensity. They spotlighted only one aspect of their characters and thus obtained powerful contrasts of light and shade.

In his lyric drama *Uroševa Ženidba*, Bojić was strongly influenced by the French playwright Edmond Rostand. This was because their dramatic concepts were similar, and because they both chose to write their plays as romantic dramas in verse, a form considered obsolete at the time. Obsolete or not, the form perfectly suited their desire for exalted lyricism and offered a way to compensate, by brilliant versification and luxurious descriptions, for the psychological oversimplification of the characters. Edmond Rostand's drama, *L'Aiglon*, is in reality Bojić's dramatic ideal incarnate. It fully develops the artistic concepts that Bojić sketched in *Uroševa Ženidba*.

The attraction Rostand and Bojić felt for the romantic drama in verse is readily comprehensible. The romantic drama in verse, compared to neo-classical tragedy, gives an almost unlimited freedom for the expression of flamboyant and uncontrolled emotionality. There is no meticulous analysis or psychological verisimilitude; it is an opening through which the illusions of poetic imagination can be dreamed out. In its versification, the Alexandrine verse of neo-classical tragedy is symmetrical and balanced, the verse of the romantic drama lyrical and flamboyant.

In Serbian romantic theater, as well as in Western romantic literature, medieval history and legends were a rich source of themes and inspiration. All Bojić's dramas, published or not, are inspired by Serbian medieval motifs.

Another characteristic of the romantic drama in verse is the fact that it is a form suited to young authors. At the first presentation of *Cyrano de Bergerac* (December 28, 1897), Rostand was only twenty-nine years old; similarly, Bojić was only twenty at the opening night of *Kraljeva Jesen*. The drama *Uroševa Ženidba* was presented after his death, but the poet was only twenty-five when he finished the manuscript. The youth of both poets shows in the emotional glitter of their dramas; without youth, there would be none of the flamboyant fireworks which are the main charm of their lyricism.

The conflict in Rostand's *L'Aiglon*[1] is basically the same as in Bojić's *Uroševa Ženidba*, that is, conflict of two diametrically opposed personalities. In *L'Aiglon*, it is the contrast between the King of Rome and the memory of his father Napoleon, in *Uroševa Ženidba*, it is the tragic difference between the emperor Dušan Silni (Dušan the Powerful) and his son Nejaki Uroš (Uroš the Weak). Such contrasts, with all the play of light and shade they afford, offered a tempting theme for young lyric poets.

Rostand influenced *Uroševa Ženidba* in both form and content. The first scene of Act III of *Uroševa Ženidba* is almost a duplicate of the first scene Act I from *L'Aiglon*. In flamboyant Alexandrines, a group of courtiers describes the protagonists and creates the atmosphere for the conflict. The many characters on stage and the intentionally segmented verses throw onto the stage the shimmering light that is one of the essential characteristics of the dramatic art of both Rostand and Bojić. The crucial lyrical monologues that these scenes introduce are a particular feature of these dramatic concepts. For the protagonists move from these group scenes into their full emotional crisis by means of monologues that the previous scenes had located in time and place. The monologues become the climax of the drama, as if the poet had superseded the playwright and as if the other scenes were merely background work.

Two arguments could be cited against such lyric drama, especially in Bojić's case. The monologues, which are the most condensed moments of the drama, are not psychologically convincing. Moreover, they burden the rhythm of the dramatic action. Their redeeming grace is their lyrical beauty, which makes them poems in themselves. Bojić's lyric dramas are still read with admiration, but they are difficult to stage properly. This is best illustration by Flambeau's famous monologue in *L'Aiglon* and Dušan's monologue in *Uroševa Ženidba.*

---

[1] The translation into Serbian of Edmond Rostand's *L'Aiglon* was presented for the first time in the National Theater in Belgrade on January 21, 1910. It was performed eleven times, which is proof of unusual success, since the theater-going public of the time was not very large. Radoslav Vesnić states, (*Venac*, Knjiga XV, 1929), that Bojić did not miss any of the eleven performances.

All their similarities notwithstanding, the two lyrical dramas differ greatly, since Rostand places the emotional accent on the weakness of the son, while Bojić stresses the powerful father, which was more in accord with his own temperamental affinities. It must also be admitted that Rostand's protagonists are better drawn, psychologically as well as dramatically.

Bojić also left translations of French poems, in which he tried to transpose French rhythm and rhymes into Serbian. His attempt was only moderately successful.

Bojić has translated the *Idol* by Auguste Barbier. In its original version, the poem has five parts written in alternating eight- and twelve-syllable verses. The rhymes are alternate. Bojić did not depart from the rhyme pattern (abab, cdcd), but was unable to transpose the alternating rhythm. All the twelve-syllable verses are preserved in the translation, but the eight-syllable verses are changed into nine-, ten-, or even twelve-syllable verses, which destroys the rhythm of the original. In short, Bojić sacrifices the versification of the French original to its meaning.

Barbier's *Idol* has 176 verses, yet Bojić's translation has only 168. This difference arises in the third part, which has 48 verses in the original and only 40 in the translation. Unfortunately, Bojić omitted the eight verses that convey the image of France and that appear the most frequently in anthologies. Not only this omission of the most important verses but also the entire translation prove once more that the Italian "tradutorre-traditorre" is true.

Though the translation of Barbier's poem is conscientious, it is important primarily because it clearly shows Bojić's taste in foreign poetry, which runs from Barbier in his extreme youth, to Hugo, Rostand and Baudelaire in his later phase.

Literatures of various countries or cultures are not strictly compartmentalized or self-sufficient. The benefits of foreign influences are enormous when transplanted rather than imitated. Bojić, like any poet, fell under such influences. But, apart from the impact of foreign influences, there also remains the question of mutual influences among the artists of one country. Here again, Bojić drew from earlier and contemporary Serbian poetic themes and forms, which he then fashioned into original works of art.

Such echoes in Bojić's poetry are frequent. Božidar Nikolajević's poem *Pozna Jesen* (Late Fall) finds a counterpart in Bojić's *Jesenje Šetnje* (Autumnal Stroll). Sometimes it is merely a similarity of motive and versification, as in Dragutin Ilić's *Judas* and Bojić's poems on Biblical themes. At other times only a single verse sounds familiar, as in:

The storm tonight will bring you my greeting. . .
(M. Bojić, Sonnet XXII)

The moon will bring you my greeting. . .
(M. Rakić, Sentimental Song)

Though these two verses are almost identical, the two poems are different in inspiration and tone.

There are echoes of Bojić's poems in the works of his contemporaries as well. Proka Jovkić, in his poem *Raspeta Zemlja* (The Crucified Country) brings Bojić's patriotic poems to mind immediately. This poem by Jovkić is also very different in form from his other poems. It is almost pure Bojić:

From your wounds blood dripped a long time
On raw wood and flagstones
In torture you died day after day
Since the beginning of your tragedy.
(P. Jovkić, The Crucified Country)

The declamatory tone and rhythm of Jovkić's poem are more than reminiscent of Bojić's style.

Bojić's aesthetic and poetic concepts are not exactly new, nor do they represent a new movement in Serbian poetry. But he was the first to introduce unveiled sensuality, a new feature that stands in sharp contrast to the romantic crooning of the late nineteenth century. Bojić's scorching sunlight is diametrically opposed to the sentimental moonlight that was then so popular.

But Bojić was not an isolated case in Serbian poetry at the beginning of the twentieth century. The poet Mirko Korolija, born in Dalmatia, reveals the same impulsive sensuality in his collection of poems published in 1914. His poetry shows the same abandon to the forces of natural instinct, the same qualities and faults as in Bojić's youthful poems. His emotions are as instinctive and ungoverned as Bojić's; they have the same flamboyant sensuality. Korolija loves nature, that is, in the same subjective way as a personal background for his fiery youth.

Korolija progressed artisitically along the same lines as Bojić. During the tragic days of World War I, he reverted to patriotic poetry as spontaneously as Bojić had. They both abandoned the passionate dithyrambs of their youth when they faced the tragedy of their nation. Korolija's youthful poems show the same lack of balance and harmony as Bojić's early poetry. It is the unavoidable consequence of their youth and passion. They both aimed at a poetry of youth, sensuality, and vitality in their attempt to rebel against the melancholy and pessimism of contemporary poets. Though there is no evidence that these two poets influenced each other, their poetic and aesthetic ideals are nevertheless quite similar.

An even more interesting fact is the similarity between the poems of Bojić and Korolija and those of the French poet Louis Payen. Vladimir Ćorović noted this in his *Preface* to Bojić's *Pesme Bola i Ponosa*: "There is in French poetry a poet who shows a kinship of inspiration with Bojić. It is Louis Payen, the poet of *Herod* and *Jason*; Emile Faguet says, speaking of Payen, that few poets sang the way he did. And Payen himself said that his heart was as fiery as a midsummer sun."

Payen was very acute in choosing the right words for his fiery imagery. His poems often have stanzas that are extremely close to those of Bojić, and the impression is the same as the one derived from Bojić's and Korolija's poems. But it is a coincidental similarity rather than an influence, since Bojić was familiar only with Payen's *Herod*, from a translation published in the literary magazine *Nova Iskra* in January 1911. The translation is in verse and signed by M. Cerić. In all the notes left by Bojić, the French poet Louis Payen is never mentioned.

Bojić was never attracted by the impersonal and cold atmosphere of the Parnassian poets. He admired Hugo's exaltation of the ego, which was much more in harmony with his romantic nature. Bojić could well have said, as Hugo does: "When I speak about myself, I am speaking really about you. Oh, unreasonable man who believes I am not you!" This romantic concept stands in contrast to Hyppolite Taine's statement: "It is in bad taste to expose one's heart. It is better to endure the reproach of not having one." Bojić's romantic concept is similar to Hugo's because, like Hugo, he willfully exalted the individual ego and all the emotions this ego experiences.

Nevertheless, Bojić was marked by the definite literary heritage the Parnassians left to French poetry. This he experienced either directly or, more often, through Rakić. From this influence comes Bojić's fascination with impeccable form, his profound awareness of the need for workmanship, and his respect for poetic language. Thus, the Parnassians influenced his form but left him cold to their artistic credo.

There is great power in Bojić's poems of pride and suffering. His personal lyrical sensitivity is devoid of melancholy and is often declamatory. It lacks the intimate tones of sadness that Velimir Rajić, for one, expressed so beautifully. But an absence of melancholy in poetry does not necessarily mean the absence of a great talent.

For Bojić, suffering never becomes melancholy; rather, it turns into pride, the force he opposed to pain. His views in this respect are controversial among his critics, who can be divided into those who liked and who did not like this particular attitude on the part of the man and the poet. Bojić, as a man and as a poet, is neither a philosopher nor a moralist. He is not concerned with social problems. He is a romantic, brilliant and enthusiastic, and, above all, a pure lyric poet. In some of his poems, especially the patriotic ones, eloquence plays a great part, but it is the eloquence of grandeur.

The imagery in Bojić's poems is mostly visual. In Dučić's poems, the visual picture is achieved through enchanting miniatures, which are often contained in barely half a verse. Bojić, on the contrary, painted vast frescoes that make up the entire poems.

The poetic work of Milutin Bojić, seen from a distance of over fifty years, undoubtedly deserves more attention than it has been given. It is to be hoped that a complete collection of his works will be published soon, for it is the lack of such a collection that impedes the reading public from gaining a full appreciation of his artistic achievements. The place he will then have in the history of Serbian poetry will not be that of a Rakić, or a Dučić, but he will definitely be one of the great poets of the twentieth century. But even now, Bojić is and will remain one of the favorite poets of the young.

MILUTIN BOJIĆ: POEMS IN TRANSLATION

(translated by Mihailo Dordević)

THE CROWS

For a long time I watched the crows flying,
Black as youth falling into an abyss.
Far away the west flared at moments,
Under grey clouds hunted by the wind.
        Without sound or aim the crows flew.

Black, all equal, they told the tragic story—
How terrifying it is to resemble the others.
Silence: mortals and eternity struggle.
The world around me falls into their net.
        How terrifying it is to resemble the others!

A cry, bursting with passion, tore the night.
The voice of a crow. The flock rushed after him.
And he cried, conscious of his powers,
And led his black brothers to their goal.
        Soundlessly the crows flew through the night.

I shivered and felt at that moment
I resembled an unknown chaste woman
Who, stepping on the path that leads to her downfall,
Shudders, while shame flushes her face.
        That night my will was born in me.

THE MARCHING

I laugh now at what childhood deplores,
Those pale days of handed-down thoughts,
Vague sorrows and unconscious longings:
Great was the day when our soul fell.

Great was the day when our soul fell,
For God cried in the core of our soul,
For destroyed was the imposed faith,
And that god appeared as the golden calf.

From that day, through squalor and swamps
Where reeds slowly rot, we sank ever deeper
With desperate screams. Bolder and tougher
We prayed with faith, each to his god.

Today a hurricane is bowing our brow,
Uncertainty fouls all our hopes,
But we keep believing a new dawn is coming,
Though our pedestal crumples under foot.

We await the doom, but from day to day,
Arrogant, we believe in sunshine and colors
And our desires, and actions, and our idols:
It is our world, perhaps false and strange.

We believe bravely to the last moment
For upon our strings the psalm is played.
While our insane youth fills us with delights,
There are less and less jewels in our crown.

The wine we thirst for turns to elusive sparkles.

AUTUMNAL STROLLS

1

More and more do I love late fall which,
All wet and grey and distorted as a ghost,
Shrinks and dims the frozen horizon
And whips the sinners who beg for mercy.

I love the call of wild ducks over waters,
And rain-soaked crows, the fog over swamps,
Oh, how infinitely I love these sad charms
When grey horizons look like somber tombs.

I stroll proud over fallen hopes,
Happy that life rots all round me,
My eyes dark but filled with sun and spring;
Then, I have neither desire nor regret.

2

The last leaves shimmer as a golden net
Over the ground and still smell
Of sunny haze that is so long gone;
They draw from earth a fresh drop of poison.

The freezing fog piously understands
This proud rest after passionate days,
This last blaze of a withering power,
The last song of my proud forest.

Dead branches are wrapped in a dense veil.
So in silence fades, without an alien tear,
This ripe song stronger than a sob:
So dies, untold, the lament of young days.

I do love this feast of twlight solitude,
When my heart is lonely and half asleep;
Then a thousand sorrows arise in me
And a string of memories dies in the dark,

Like the perfume of a woman slowly disappearing.

THE LEGEND OF THE WOMAN

Sleepy earth breathed its purple vapors,
Blue evergreens lowered their heads,
Over dead seas crows were crying sadly,
The Southern sun was melting in a golden bronze.

The burning sand glared and shimmered;
Tearing the skies, tall mountains slept;
On the red beach dreamed a flock of cranes,
Flies were dancing over the river.

Hot, drowsy in the music of peace and colors,
Bored, man watched this luxury.
He lay bloody, a mess of hair and sweat,
And tried to see himself in the sunny rays.

The ripe hour of the day was empty.
Man waited for a form new,
A thing lush, sunny, like sea foam.
Suddenly he laughed with throaty passion.

Down evergreen slopes came the woman.

THE KISS

We were born to be happy, to love life fully;
Our love is bizarre, naked and coarse,
And we hate those born for frozen nights;
Youth is our god, and passion our strength.

. . . . January storms howl through frozen eventide,
And whip the river into ice-blue froth,
While moaning trees arouse the dead:
Bitter is the laughter of vanishing time.

The world is a clash of conflicting wills:
Bellows and screams, thunders and death.
While rabid gales tear the skies apart,
Frozen tides duel with burning hell!

Intoxicated with hatred, surrounded by screams,
In a sensual kiss our bleeding lips are glued,
And strong ribs strain under the pressure
Of unconscious fingers that grip them with passion.

In that kiss we exchange our burning souls.
Myriads of ambers and glowing cinders
Dance and flash as the eyes of tigers,
While grey skies are turning pale blue.

Then I see flocks of scared fawns dashing,
Staring like rabbits with terrified eyes,
Chanting psalms of an unknown religion
Buried deep in their childlike gaze.

For centuries already they've snickered like that.
Unseen their rabble swarms the universe;
For to see them we need our hearts to bleed
And echo their fear and thus bring them to life.

DESTINY

Perchance you anticipated the hateful arena
To see my defeat and the thumbs-down sign,
But I am unconscious to the lauding of women
And refuse to know failure or regret.

Blood-soaked is the sand, and foaming mouths,
Crackling of flames, burning resin in skins,
Rows of public moving like waves on sea
Wherever my blow or naked feet dash:

For I don't present the view of a rotten feast
Where made-up faces watch through an emerald
The lightening of a sword, the swell of a silk dress
On which the name of a loser is a splash of mud.

My arrogant fight is the scream of life.
Unnamed but accustomed to fight, my shoulder
Is not for parade arms and amusement:
Centuries watched me carry this fight.

The millstones of countless invasions didn't grind me.
I am not bewildered by pain, nor tired by that sight.
I am the father and the son of a bleeding crowd,
I adorn myself with oak and not with lily.

For a kiss I shall repay with my own Golgotha;
For a blow I shall sink my teeth in your very heart
And once done I'll assist the ravaged enemy;
I have learned to laugh through my sobs.

A chalice perhaps for many, it is surely mine
And I don't boast of knowing how to drink it,
Maybe all races intermingled speak through me,
Or unfathomable I am just myself.

SELF-AWARENESS

Be proud when the last judgment comes,
And Satan appears to select the sinners.
Through their empty skulls he will howl with delight
And devastate gardens that were filled with flowers.

Be proud then of the ancient and heroic times
When from the cradle all cried in killing,
When you waited for a God with an olive branch
In the frozen despair of all-embracing doom.
Be proud because you are the fury of a dying storm
And your fate will be told with titanic words;
To conquer all you must relinquish all;
It is by giving away heaven that world was made.

Be proud, for centuries will remember your name,
And on your grave your sons will dream,
And on your head as your most sainted halo
Will lie your battle-whitened hair.

THE SNOWSTORM

Endless and white rests the plain;
Petrified soldiers like frozen heroes
Their laurels buried under the white shroud.
All is quiet while awaiting a curse!

Through the dead silence of oaks and pines
The death toll is muted and cannot be heard.
Grey mountains rise like tombstones
And glaciers bathe in ashen fog.

Days have passed but nothing is changed;
Not a cry nor a sob in the tragic twilight,
Not even a smile on that dead sky.

Midday, midnight are equal in deafness.
Faced with such pain gods have retreated
From this hell into their abyss.

Snowflakes fall relentlessly from the white chasm.

BEFORE THE PROMISED LAND

As if facing the gates of old Canaan
A nation stands that refused temptation,
Stern as the Cedars of antique Lebanon,
Calm as a congregation at a solemn mass.

In those serene eyes shines the reflection
Of ancient cities, proud mountains and seas.
Men's brows are furrowed with agony and pain,
Their lips sealed in silent thunder and threat.

Under steel helmets their eyes are tense
With frozen decision to return North.
Shriveled fingers are like tiger's claws
Their blood boiling with deadly resolve.

Steeped in suffering, with inflexible faith,
They feel history ready to beat in their breast,
While they soak their iron pens in blood
And chase the enemy that drove them here.

Their death kiss will bring destruction,
Their embrace will warm bodies to life
So they may sleep without burning dreams:
Sleep and never wake from their final rest.

They wait for great days which are coming,
Those same men who outlasted deaths,
Snows and winds and were not destroyed.
As if facing the gates of old Canaan
Highly strung they wait for your call, my Lord!

THE SEA GRAVE

Hold Imperial galleons! Stay your oars,
        Proceed with calm,
In these holy waters, I say a proud mass
        In midnight horror.

Beneath the sea, on sleeping shells
And weeds which gently fall,
Lies a grave of heroes, brother next to brother,
Prometheuses of hope, apostles of tragedy.

Don't you feel how gently the sea swells
Not to disturb their eternal rest?
From the deep a sense of peace prevails,
While an exhausted moon gazes at the sea.

This mysterious temple, this tragic grave
For a common corpse unified in thought,
Is calm as midnight over a south island
Yet cold and desperate like a man's conscious.

Can't you feel from these blue depths
That piety rules these seas
And the air is rife with mystery?
The souls of heroes walk the seas.

Hold Imperial galleons! Over my fallen brothers
Muffle your trumpets in black!
And let men-at-arms sing the mass
Here where the waves lap the bows.

For many centuries will pass
Like waves which rule the seas,
And a new generation will build a house
Of glory over these very graves.

But this grave in which lies
The tragic mystery of an epic deed
Will cradle immortal glory
For future times to come.

Resting here are laurels of the past
And the shattered joys of a nation
In this somber grave under blue waves
Between the earth and sky.

Hold Imperial galleons! Snuff out your torches,
Cease the splashing of your oars,
When my mass is said, glide into the night
In piety and silence.

For I want serenity and quiet to rule
For the dead to hear the battles of the living,
And heed the boiling turmoil of their sons
Under the wings of victory.

There, far away, the battlefields are flooded
With the same blood that is at rest here:
Here peace reigns over the fathers,
While sons there make history.

That's why I crave peace for this requiem,
Without words, tears, or weak sighs,
To unite the clouds of incense and gunpowder
With the muted rumbling of drums.

Hold Imperial galleons! In the name of respect
Glide without a sound.
I say a requiem like the heavens have yet to hear
Over these holy waters.

THE SOWERS

Akin to erring knights haunted by a curse
From far away south, sharing the fate of Job,
Now we come to you, our freezing brother,
Proud, though we have no kinfolk nor roof:
Intrepid we shall face new cemeteries.

Through centuries we refused to gauge our blood;
The plains of Ankara are still steeped in it,
The chasms of Karst drank it freely,
It shamed the walls of Adrianopolis
Revenging the wounds of Pannonian plains.

But still we sow our bones lavishly
Through islands and foreign waters,
Through deserts and howling simoons
And frozen steppes. And at eventide
Gorged with blood vultures leave our bodies.

Ancient fires, now dead under ashes,
Are silent as old forgotten memories.
Still alive we leave our dead there,
Like the wandering Jew pursued by the curse of God,
Our eyes roam over endless plains.

All the universe became our infinite field
For this seed of honor which will grow to the sun.
Oh, Lord, did you not punish us enough?
It is harvest time, time to cut the wheat,
Time to raise the stone that covers the tomb.

As wanderers haunted by endless suffering,
From the mellow south, sharing the fate of Job,
Now we come to you, our freezing brother;
Proud, though we have no kinfolk nor roof:
Intrepid we shall face new cemeteries.

WITHOUT FATHERLAND

One thought wakes us in the morning,
One thought fills all our days,
One thought destroys the peace of our nights:
How does father endure?

One worry rouses us as a death sentence,
One worry dodges our steps all day,
One worry gnaws at our heart all night:
Is mother still alive?

One longing wakes us at daybreak,
One longing lies in the heart all day,
One longing burns in the heart all day:
How is my wife?

One fear wakes us as a requiem,
One fear drives us blind with pain,
One fear distills hatred all night:
Are the sisters abused?

One torture as a clarion announces the day,
One torment we drink in every chalice,
One anguish tears the breast apart:
Where are my children?

One road only leads to the answer
Across a bridge of corpses over our blood;
Then you will reach home where mother
Overwhelmed awaits her son.

UNTOLD THOUGHTS

Oh, God of my fathers, Lord of my children,
Why abandon me and destroy all I had?
Our churches toll dead instead of hours,
And at your altar my heart is bleeding.

My cities are nothing but heaps of ruins,
My barns are bare, my palaces adorned in black,
Executioners are beheading men along my roads,
In my home the sacred light is extinguished.

Oh, God of my fathers, do you see my daughters?
For the feats of enemies they are like fruit and wine;
If I have sinned, let not their chastity atone;
Cover with plague their breasts and lips,

Make them hideous so that their pure bodies
Don't serve as drinking cups to the enemy;
Turn them into horrors and nightmare visions
With monstrous laughter driving their foe away.

Don't allow innocent children to grow in despair
Cursing their mother's womb and their day of birth;
Give them peaceful sleep after forlorn days,
Let them not repudiate their fathers' blood.

Don't let our fathers betray their sons,
Nor disavow their blood and bury all their hopes!
Men are dying, Satan is calling for me:
God, let me in my agony keep believing in you.

WOMEN

In a graveyard a group of prowling women
Treads silently not to wake the dead;
In long lines they string yellow candles:
Winter winds howl over the city.

Petrified and mute they face the crosses;
Night and cold creep into their bones,
But what do they care for night and cold
When the passing of time has lost its meaning.

Not a sound, not a movement among them;
Frozen tears stopped flowing on their cheeks;
Not a sigh to bring this scene to life:
Petrified, two worlds confront each other.

Only winds are howling the despair
Buried in the soul of these women.
From one mountain to another echoes:
—They are great as they always were.

SONNET I

Oh, it's an old story: we all wear masks,
We are all actors for better or worse:
God gave us a lie to worship as an idol—
With senseless sounds we roar on that stage.

But today I saw the boards on which
Truth spoke clearly, I thought,
Where bright and high was burning its torch
And where despised was all worldly praise:

Today I witnessed the fall of the idol!
Erased is the gilt, white flash the bones,
Under the laurels I saw the shroud

And all the snakes leering from that grave.
I learned the horror of the unremitting fall:
On that stage I was acting, even when alone.

SONNET II

Why are you not that all-embracing woman,
The goal of my thoughts and desire,
Who could in a whim condemn, destroy me,
She who takes all, but whom we forgive?

Your perfume would lull my sorrows to sleep,
To dreams from which, alas, I would wake
To raging storms and the dreadful cold
In which the dust of stars is but vanity.

Force me not on new roads; grant me peace!
Force me not to new lies told in new temples;
My soul fears its own destiny,

For it sees itself forever barren, lonely,
As Ahasfer sentenced to wander forever,
Cursed by all those it so craves to love.

SONNET III

For then I saw the world in you:
Sisters, mother, the sun, and all
Sounds and colors, the words and the foam,
Your thought was woven into my breath.

And that's why I don't want sadness
Nor the nostalgia of wilting flowers.
You, like a dreamy haze, are all my beauty,
Though there is no passion left for you.

Fade away, thus, translucent and dreamy
For me to remember always the same:
As an icon to protect me from all evil.

Break into a myriad of shiny stars. . .
Oh, stay like this, glittering and pure.
Why couldn't you be the all-embracing woman?

SONNET V

I leaf through your letters today, my love,
And listen to your giggles of childlike innocence
And pure love; and the warmth of your budding youth:
I read your letters and fall prey to despair.

For bygone days fell over them in thick layers,
And they contain the sadness of all that once was:
Remember the days of passionate longings?
There now lies buried a flock of pure white birds.

The flight that flew through night and silence!
I can still hear their wings flapping across the sky.
Tonight they fly only over shallow graves.

Their echo is frozen and softly on your letters fall
Wings that fell off our dead butterflies;
And while memory blindly tries to wake your letters,
I so want our birds to fly free again.

SONNET VII

I took my dreams and created an aura about you
But I do not regret it had to be so;
I know I used lies to weave my dreams:
Yes, those were dreams but of great delight.

When rain washes away gilt from the gods,
There will remain a touching, sweet memory,
The beat of your young heart that expressed
Your own desires and your young volition.

And when your smile and youth fade away
And your whole being dissolves in the past,
And even the tears we shed are forgotten

And I start laughing at those tender days,
I shall hear mount like the sap in a spring tree
The beat of your trusting heart.

SONNET VIII

You are flowing from her, you, my sun ray,
You touched, caressed her hair;
Though unconscious of all her beauty,
You gathered your light from her eyes.

When you shine, sun ray, you don't know
That you are only reflecting her sad smile,
That smile which my soul needs so,
Oh, sun ray, I need you to touch my face.

You sparkle in all your golden dust
Representing her smile and the perfume of her,
I need you to penetrate my soul.

Don't throw elsewhere your ephemeral splendour,
Spread instead strong roots in me;
Stay, I beg you, you don't know all you are.

SONNET X

You are the shrine of all my youth,
Sunny mornings and scorching noons:
Buried in you is my innocent love
And petals from our wilted flowers.

Time has come for requiems and mournful chants,
They permeate me with wisps of autumnal fog,
Plains and rocks cry around me exhausted
And shadows encompass all that once was bright.

Are you not proud as a priceless urn
That contains the remnants of dead kings?
But no: You are sad! And you blush with shame.

I understand! With the night of fire and passion
We tried to bring back the flames of past days,
And resurrect in us the long dead gods.

Midnight. The last star has just died.

SONNET XIII

We shall meet again in a winter day,
In a foggy twilight, wrought with dead hopes;
You will not be young, nor passionate,
But still conscious of all that once lived.

Your old smile will shine and with it
You will bring back the past, the masquerade
Of bygone kisses, dreams, and serenades
Will flutter again on newborn wings.

But just for a moment. And then
In our eyes will lie the corpse of May.
That one fleeting smile will tell

That dead is the life we loved so.
What we used to call our whole life
Was just a small, brilliant part.

SONNET XIV

I searched for a whole new sky
In which to pour my soul and dreams,
A soul made of shallow tides and dreams,
A soul despairing in empty lies.

You, with your garland of weak desires,
The sighs you breathed through endless nights,
Songs you heard from Satan and angels,
You longed to blend them into one, dreamy me.

We both craved for the same idol
And led by the Vague, we both erred,
As if looking for each other in the dark.

At our first meeting we uttered a word
We had never said before. As though unaware,
Not knowing it, we already loved.

SONNET XVI

I recall that winter morning: your eyes,
Tearful, searching the depth of mine;
For you wanted to see, deep in me,
Was it love, or was I just acting.

You looked deep, deep. The dawn broke
But I saw your eyes, once bold and free,
Beg in humble surrender. All was silence.
And all was quiet. Only the rustle of trees.

Away from you now I still see your eyes,
And if I wanted to forget even your name,
That sadness in your eyes would still live in me.

I cannot even sin as I used to sin before.
. . . Strange is that love which holds our hearts:
Now that I love you, I dread your sad eyes.

UNPUBLISHED POEM, UNTITLED

Like a dead body without will or strength
I neither hear, nor see, nor feel any more.
Black raindrops are singing above my head
The deep pain born from happy memories.

Boredom with her retinue of sadness
Tortures me and burns like poison.
Dead are my faith and self-assurance,
My brow is creased and furrowed by worries.

Everything in me cries and laments;
I am mortified for there is no more
Strength left in my heart, only death
Where once were melodies of happy days.

I don't even know how to laugh any more,
My own words are painful and consume me.
Oh, my spring, death is, death is near.
Fog and incense are all around me.

(Last known poem written by M. Bojić, 1917)

BIBLIOGRAPHY

ARNAUTOVIĆ, ALEXANDER. "La Renaissance de notre poésie romantique," *La Patrie Serbe*, Année I, Paris (1917).

BANJAC, DJURO. "Pesme Bola i Ponosa," *Beogradski Dnevnik*, knjiga I, br. 51, (29 novembar 1919).

BOGDANOVIĆ, DAVID. *Pregled Književnosti Hrvatske i Srpske*, Zagreb, (1926).

BOGDANOVIĆ, MILAN. "Frane Supilo et Milutin Bojić à la Yougoslavie" *La Patrie Serbe*, knjiga I, Paris, (1917).

BOJIĆ, RADIVOJE. "Milutin Bojić, pesnik Srbije," Windsor, Canada, Avala Press, (1968).

BOŽOVIĆ, BRANKO. "Kraljeva Jesen od Milutina Bojića," *Pijemont*, (1913).

ĆOROVIĆ, VLADIMIR. "Predgovor uz zbirku Pesme i Drame," Beograd, (1927).

ĆOROVIĆ, VLADIMIR. "M. Bojić," *Književni Jug*, knjiga I, (1918).

CVETKOVIĆ, SAVA. "M. Bojić, desetogodišnjica pesnikove smrti," *Novosti*, broj 2058, (9 novembar 1927).

CVIJANOVIĆ, S. B. "Beleška uz zbirku Pesme Bola i Ponosa," Beograd, (1920).
"Desetogodisnjica Milutina Bojića," *Reč*, br. 1084 (1927).
"Desetogodisnjica Milutina Bojića," *Volja*, knjiga III (1927).

DJURIĆ, MILOŠ. "Na grobu Milutina Bojića," *Reč*, br. 1085, (dec. 1918).

DORNIS, JEAN. "Jedan srpski pesnik: Milutin Bojić," preveo A. Arnautović, *Zabavnik Srpskih Novina*, br. 17, (15 oktobar 1918).

DZONIĆ, UROŠ. "M. Bojić," *Ilustrovani List*, knjiga I, br. 1, (1919).

FILIPOVIĆ, DRAGOLJUB. "M. Bojić," *Zabavnik Srpskih Novina*, br. 7, (15 novembar 1917).

FILIPOVIĆ, DRAGOLJUB. "M. Bojić, predgovor Kraljevoj Jeseni," Sarajevo, (1918).

GLIGORIĆ, VELIBOR. "Naša istoriska drama, M. Bojić," *Raskrsnica*, knjiga II, br. 10, (1924).

GROL, MILAN. "Svetli grobovi," *Prosveta, almanah za godinu 1918*, Ženeva, (1918).

IBROVAC, MIODRAG. "Veče posvećeno pesniku Pesama Bola i Ponosa," *Politika*, (29 decembar 1937).

IBROVAC, MIODRAG. "M. Bojić: Soneti," *Srpski Književni Glasnik*, knjiga V *Nova Serija*, (1922).

ILIĆ, ALEKSANDAR. "Rostan i Bojić," *Novi Život*, knjiga XVI, (1924).

JANKOVIĆ, VELMAR. "M. Bojic: Pesme i Drame," *Novi Vidici*, knjiga I, (1928).

JOVANOVIĆ, SLOBODAN. "Jedan tužan datum. Dvadesetpetogodišnjica smrti M. Bojića," *Srpska Scena*, br. 16, (1942).

JOVANOVIĆ, SLOBODAN. "Uroševa ženidba. Pred našu novu premijeru," *Srpska Scena*, br. 11-12, (1944).

KAŠANIN, MILAN. "M. Bojić," *Savremenik*, knjiga XIV, (1918).

KIĆOVIĆ, MIRAŠ. "Neobjavljeni članak o nepoznatoj Bojićevoj drami," Manuscript, not published.
"Književno veče u spomen Milutina Bojića," *Politika*, (Decembar 1937).
"Kostimologija Uroševe Ženidbe," *Komedija*, I, br. 4, (1923).

KOVIJANIĆ, GAVRILO. "Život i književni rad Milutina Bojića," Beograd, *Naučna Knjiga*, (1969).

KRKLEC, GUSTAV. "M. Bojić, na nemačkom," *Srpski Književni Glasnik*, Nova Serija knjiga VII, (1922).

KRUNIĆ, DUŠAN. "M. Bojić: Uroševa Ženidba," *Pravda*, (13 decembar 1922).

KRŠIĆ, JOVAN. "Listak na grob pesniku M. Bojiću," *Politika*, (19 april 1930).

KRŠIĆ, JOVAN. "Nepoznata pesma Bojićeva: Zelene Oči," *Srpski Književni Glasnik*, Nova Serija, knjiga XXX, (1930).

LAZAREVIĆ, BRANKO. "Pesme M. Bojića," *Letopis Matice Srpske*, knjiga 298, (1914).

LJUMOVIĆ, KRSTA. "Štampane drame M. Bojića," *Zapisi*, knjiga I, (1927).
"M. Bojić," Pozorišni Godišnjak, službeno izdanje, (1923-24).

MARKOVIĆ, MILAN. "Uroševa Ženidba, komedija u tri čina u stihovima od Milutina Bojića," *Venac*, knjiga IX, (1924).

MARTINOVIĆ, ALEKSANDAR. "Pesme Bola i Ponosa, M. Bojić," *Zapisi*, knjiga VIII, (1931).

MICIĆ, R. "M. Bojić, Soneti." *Budućnost*, knjiga II, (1922).

MILAČIĆ, DUŠAN. "M. Bojić, lirski pesnik. Esej." *Misao*, knjiga II, sveska 5, (1920).
"Milutin Bojić: Kraljeva Jesen," *Delo*, knjiga 69 (1913).
"Milutin Bojić: Pesme," *Delo*, knjiga 70 (1914).
"Milutin Bojić," *Politika* (9 novembar 1927).
"Milutin Bojić. Povodom prenosa kostiju našeg rano preminulog pesnika," *Novosti*, br. 439, (18 oktobar 1922).
"Milutin Bojić," *Vardar Kalendar*, knjiga XXIX, (1939).
"Milutin Bojić," *Vreme*, (17 oktobar 1922).

MITROPAN, PETAR. "M. Bojić, Soneti." *Južna Srbija*, knjiga VIII, (1931).

MLADENIVIĆ, RANKO; "Gizdava komika u nacionalnoj drami: Premijera Uroševe Ženidbe," *Komedija*, kniga I, br. 3, (1923).
"Naš kvatroćento u nacionalnoj drami—povodom premijere Uroševe Ženidbe," *Trgovinski glasnik*, br. 284 (9 decembar 1923).

NIKOLIĆ, DRAGOSLAV. "M. Bojić, pesnik bola i ponosa." *Duga*, knjiga VII, br. 283, (1951).

NOVAKOVIĆ, BOŠKO. "Poezija M. Bojića." *Misao*, knjiga XXXIV, (1930).
"O Uroševoj Ženidbi," *Srpski Scena*, knjiga III, br. 11-12, (1944).

PETROVIĆ, NIKOLA. "Pesnik našeg izgnanstva. Pomen M. Bojiću povodom prenosa njegovih kostiju u otažbinu." *Venac*, knjiga VIII, (1922).

PETROVIĆ, SVETOSLAV. "Uroševa Ženidba od Milutina Bojića." *Srpski Književni Glasnik*, Nova Serija, knjiga XI, (1924).

PEŠIĆ, MIRODRAG. "Neobjavljene pesme M. Bojića." *Volja*, knjiga I, (1926).
"Pesnik Bojić," *Novosti*, br. 438 (17 oktobar 1922).

POPOVIĆ, DJORDJE. "Ljubavi srpskih pisaca." *Biblioteka Život*. Gradina, (1975).

PREDIĆ, MILAN. "Kraljeva Jesen od Milutina Bojića." *Srpski Književni Glasnik*, knjiga XXXI, (1913).
"Premijera Uroševe Ženidbe," *Trgovački Glasnik*, (14 decembar 1923).

RISTIĆ, KOSTA. "M. Bojić, Soneti," *Letopis Matice Srpske*, knjiga 301, (1923).

RISTIĆ, MILOVAN. "Sećanje na Milutina Bojića na dan desetogodišnjice njegove smrti sa neobljavljenim stihovima." *Pravda*, (8 nov. 1927).

SEKULIĆ, ISIDORA. "Beleske o M. Bojiću." *Srpski Književni Glasnik*, Nova Serija, knjiga 44, (1935).

SEKULIĆ, ISIDORA. "M. Bojić." *Vreme*, (22 novembar 1934).

ŠIJAČKI, DUŠAN. "M. Bojić, žrtve srpske knjige 1915-1918" *Vidovdan, illustrovana istorija srpskih ratova 1912-1918*. Ženeva, (1918).
"Srpsko Pozorište: Uroševa Ženidba, drama M. Bojića" *Komedija*, knjiga II, br. 5, (29 decembar 1924).

STEVOVSKI, M. "Premijera Uroševe Ženidbe u Beogradskom Pozorištu." *Komedija*, knjiga I, br. 5, (17 decembar 1923).

ST–C, ST. "Uspomene na Bojića." *Sad i Nekad*, knjiga II, br. 8, (1937).

ŠUMAREVIĆ, SVETISLAV. "M. Bojić." *Pozorište kod Srba*, Beograd, (1938).
"Svečana pretstava prilikom 25-godišnjice smrti Milutina Bojića," *Srpska Scena*, knjiga 1, br. 16, (1942).

TALETOV, PETAR. "Kraljeva Jesen, drama u jednom činu od M. Bojića," *Delo*, knjiga 49 (1913).
"Tri neštampane pesme M. Bojića," *Srpski Književni Glasnik*, Nova Serija, knjiga IV, (1921).
"M. Bojić, Soneti," *Novi Život*, knjiga IX, (1922).
"Uroševa Ženidba od Milutina Bojića," *Srpski Književni Glasnik*, Nova Serija, knjiga V, (1921).

U.V.B. "Pesme M. Bojića," *Srpski Književni Glasnik*, knjiga LIII, (1938).

VESNIĆ, RADOSLAV. "Slepi Despot–neobljavljena drama Milutina Bojića." *Venac*, knjiga XV, (1929).

VINAVER, STANISLAV. "Skerlić i Bojić," *Pravda*, (brojevi od 6, 9, i 10 januara 1935 i od 6 aprila 1935).

VUKOVIĆ, VLADETA. "Književno delo Milutina Bojića." *Zajednica Naučnih Ustanova Kosova*, Priština, (1969).

VUKOVIĆ, VLADETA. "Pesnik Bola i Ponosa. Povodom 60-godisnjice rodjenja Bojića." *Stvaranje*, knjiga VII, br. 4, (1954).

VULOVIĆ, ZORA. "Milutin Bojić." *Glasnik Profesorskog Drustva*, knjiga II, (1922).

ZAHAROV, LAV. "Poezija M. Bojića." *Republika*, (8 april 1952).

ŽIVADINOVIĆ, STOJAN. "M. Bojić." *Venac*, knjiga IX, (1924).

ŽIVALJEVIĆ, DIMITRIJE. "M. Bojić." *Budućnost*, knjiga II, (1922).

ŽIVANOVIĆ, JEREMIJA. "Jedna desetogodišnjica." *Venac*, knjiga XIII (1927).

ŽIVANOVIĆ, JEREMIJA. "M. Bojić." *Venac*, knjiga VII, (1921).

ŽIVANOVIĆ, JEREMIJA. "Prerani pokojnici," *Venac*, knjiga VIII, (1922).

GLOSSARY

ADAM, PAUL (1862-1920). French writer. Some of his early works were influenced by both Naturalism and Symbolism, and represent an original blend of these rival movements.

ALBANIAN EXODUS (also known as the SERBIAN GOLGOTHA). The two month retreat of the Serbian army in the winter of 1915 (November and December) through the snow storms and ice of the Albanian mountains. The seventy-one year old King Peter I, seriously ill and exhausted, was driven across the Albanian mountains on an ox-drawn cart, while the fatally ill Field Marshall, Radomir Putnik, was carried by his men on an improvised sedan chair to die in France in 1917. An estimated 100,000 died before reaching the Adriatic Sea, where another estimated 20,000 died on the islands of Corfu and Vido. At the beginning of the war (August, 1914), the Serbian army totaled approximately 400,000; but after the Albanian Exodus, the surviving army transferred to Corfu represented about 160,000 men.

D'ANNUNZIO, GABRIELE (1864-1938). (Pseudonym, Duca Minimo; title, Prince of Monte Nevosa; original surname, Rapagnetta). Italian poet, novelist, and politician (Fascist). He was one of the leaders of the Italian Nationalist school; his style was rich and flowing.

BARBIER, AUGUSTE (1805-1882). French writer and poet. He enjoyed great fame in his time, primarily known as the author of *Iambes* and *The Idol*.

BARRÈS, MAURICE (1862-1923). French novelist, journalist and politician. Author of *Les Déracinés, La Colline inspirée, L'Amitié dans les tranchées,* and *La Croix de Guerre*.

BAUDELAIRE, CHARLES (1821-1867). French poet, critic, and moralist. His chief work is the collection of poems, *Les Fleurs du mal* (1857), for which he was prosecuted. He influenced the Symbolists both through his own approach to writing and technique, and by his theory (formulated in the sonnet, "Correspondances") that all arts are one and are a manifestation of the universal essence.

BERGSON, HENRI (1859-1941). French philosopher. The most influential of modern temporalistic, antimechanistic thinkers, his basic ideas (especially through their influence on Proust) reached a very wide public. His system rests on the liberation of mental intuitions from the idea of space and the scientific notion of time, and on the affirmation of an "élan vital," a creative life-force.

BEŠEVIĆ, STEVAN (1868-1942). Serbian poet associated with the humoristic-satirical journal, *Vrač-Pogadjač*.

CAMBLAK, GRIGORIJE (b. 1365, d. Kiev, 1419 or 1420). Born in Bulgaria, educated in Constantinople, he lived and worked among Bulgarians, Serbs, Rumanians, and Russians. In 1415, he became the Metropolitan of Kiev. He wrote a biography of Stephan Dečanski (1403-1404), son of King Milutin.

CARTESIAN. Term coined after the name of Descartes, René (1596-1650), French philosopher, physicist and mathematician, who founded modern metaphysics, rejecting scholasticism and providing the method of reasoning generally called Cartesianism.

CHATEAUBRIAND, Vte FRANCOIS RENÉ de (1768-1848). French author and statesman. His most famous works were *Le Génie du Christianisme* (1802), in which he emphasized the aesthetic and human appeal of Christianity, and *Mémoires d'outre-tombe*, a passionate autobiography.

CHENIER, ANDRÉ MARIE de (1762-1794). French poet, often considered the greatest of 18th century French poets. At first inspired by the classics, he later showed strong romantic feeling, especially in *La jeune captive*. He was guillotined and most of his work was published posthumously.

ĆIPIKO, IVO (1896-1923). Novelist born in Dalmatia. In 1912, he moved to Serbia. He wrote a number of short stories and two novels describing the life and local charm of Dalmatian fishing villages and small towns.

COLERIDGE, SAMUEL TAYLOR (1772-1834). Famous English Romantic poet and critic, and friend of Wordswoth. Later in his career he concentrated on philosophy, politics, theology and criticism.

CORNEILLE, PIERRE (1606-1684). French poet and playwright. The main theme of his tragedies is a conflict betwen honor and love. His main works are *Le Cid* (1636), *Polyeucte* (1641), *Cinna* (1641) and *Horace* (1640).

ĆOROVIĆ, SVETOZAR (1875-1919). Serbian writer from Mostar (Herzegovina). He wrote novels and dramas, and published collected stories. Together with A. Šantić and J. Dučić, Ćorović founded the literary journal, *Zora*.

ĆOROVIĆ, VLADIMIR (1885-1941). Historian and, from 1919, professor at the University of Belgrade. Born in a patriotic family in Mostar (Herzegovina), he belonged to the national youth movement in Bosnia and Herzegovina—Mlada Bosna. In 1914, after the assassination of Crown Prince Ferdinand in Sarajevo, he was accused of treason and jailed with other members of the youth movement. Following his pardon in 1917, he moved to Zagreb and collaborated on the literary journal, *Književni Jug* (The Literary South). He was a member of the National State Council for Bosnia and Herzegovina which took an active part in the proclamation of the Kingdom of Serbs, Croats and Slovenes (see also WORLD WAR I—SERBIA).

ĆURČIN, MILAN (1880-?). Serbian poet, journalist, and publisher. From 1907-14, he was an assistant professor at the University of Belgrade. One of the first Serbian poets who wrote in free verse, B. Popović in his *Anthology* gives Ćurčin a leading place in the modern trends of poetry. Between World War I and II, he published the review, *Nova Evropa* in Zagreb.

DANILO II (+1337) Fourteenth-century Serbian Archbishop and chronicler, who played an important role in the political life of medieval Serbia. Danilo built several monasteries and wrote about the lives of Serbian monks. He is the basic literary source for the Serbian history of the period from 1270 to 1335.

DANTE ALIGHIERI (1265-1321). Italian poet. Because of his involvement in the Guelf-Ghibelline wars, he spent his life from 1301 in exile in France. His *Commedia* (1308-1320), not called *Divina* until the 16th century, is an imaginary journey through Hell, Purgatory, and Paradise, and symbolizes the path of the soul from sin and darkness to purification.

DELO. Literary and scientific journal published monthly from 1894 to 1914, in Belgrade.

DE QUINCEY, THOMAS (1785-1859). English critic and essayist, who is best known for his *Confessions of an English Opium Eater* (1821). His recollections of his literary contemporaries (especially Wordsworth, Coleridge, and Southey) are valuable.

DJURADJ BRANKOVIĆ, Despot (1427-1456). He was the last Serbian ruler, having lost his sovereignty to the Ottoman Turks in 1456. The Ottoman rule lasted until the uprisings in the nineteenth century and the eventual liberation of Serbia.

DOMANOVIĆ, RADOJE (1873-1908). Serbian novelist, author of a number of realistic and pessimistic stories about village life, as well as of political satires.

DRINA. River separating Bosnia from Serbia. In 1914, it was the frontier between the Austro-Hungarian Monarchy and the Kingdom of Serbia.

DUČIĆ, JOVAN (1872-1943). Serbian poet and diplomat born in Herzegovina. Recognized as a promising poet, Dučić was helped by Serbian literary circles to leave his early work as a village teacher and was sent to study in Paris. Later he entered the diplomatic service, eventually reaching the rank of Royal Ambassador. His brilliant and elegant style was developed under the fluence of French poetry (Parnassians to Symbolists, especially A. Samain); Dučić and his diplomatic colleague, Milan Rakić, are considered the greatest Serbian poets of the twentieth century and played the most important role in the development of Serbian poetry. Dučić died during World War II in the United States and is buried at the Saint Sava's Orthodox Monastery in Libertyville, Illinois.

DUŠAN THE MIGHTY (STEPHEN DUŠAN). Serbian king (1331-1345) and emperor (1345-1355). Most powerful of the Serbian medieval rulers, his realm stretched from the Gulf of Corinth in the south, to the Danube River in the north, and from the Aegean to the Adriatic coasts. He was crowned Emperor of Serbs and Greeks.

FAGUET, EMILE (1874-1916). Author of voluminous French literary history and essays. He was a professor of literature at the Sorbonne.

FILIPOVIĆ, DRAGOLJUB (1884-1933). Serbian patriotic poet. His poetic collection, *Kosovski božuri* (The Peonies of Kossovo), is based on the story of the battle of Kossovo (1389) and its heroes. Every spring, the Kossovo plain is covered with peonies blooming in two colors. Legend has it that the red flowers represent the blood of the Serbian soldiers who fell in battle and the blue peonies represent the blood of the fallen Turks.

FORT, PAUL (1872-1960). French Symbolist poet and dramatist, author of *Ballades françaises*.

FRANCE, ANATOLE (1844-1924). French novelist and critic, he wrote an elegant, classical French. His works include *Le Crime de Sylvestre Bonnard, Les Dieux ont soif*. His works inspired by World War I were *Ce que disent les morts* and *Sur la voie de la gloire*.

GAUTHIER, THÉOPHILE (1811-1872). French poet, journalist and novelist. As a young man, he was a violent Romantic, evolving to a refined Parnassian. His best verse appeared in *Emaux et Camées* (1852). He also wrote numerous novels and books of travel, as well as literary, dramatic and art criticism.

GLIŠIC, MILOVAN (1887-1908). Serbian Realist author, who wrote novels depicting village life, and also translated into Serbian Russian classics, such as the works of Tolstoy and Gogol.

GOETHE, JOHANN WOLFGANG VON (1749-1832). German poet, dramatist, and novelist. He freed the German language from its heaviness and foreign literary domination in a vast output of easy, natural, and personal lyrics, inspiring great German composers. As a playwright, Goethe is most famous for his *Faust* (1808 and 1832). As a novelist, he influenced a generation of German writers with his *Sorrows of Werther* (1774) and the *Wilhelm Meister* novels (1796-1829).

GOURMONT, REMY de (1858-1915). French critic and novelist. He was the first to draw attention to the importance of the Symbolist writers.

HAUPTMANN, GERHARDT (1862-1946). German dramatist, representative of the German Naturalistic School and author of *Till Eulenspiegel* (1928). Hautpmann was long regarded as the father of modern German literature. His first work was a romantic epic, *Promethidenlos* (The Lot of the Promethides, 1885) His most socially prominent play was *The Weavers*. He was awarded the Nobel Prize for literature in 1912.

HEINE, HEINRICH (1797-1856). German Romantic poet. His lyric poetry, *Buch der Lieder* (1827) combines vivid natural imagery with a mixture of sentiment and irony. Many of his poems were set to music, especially by Schubert and Schumann. His prose reveals a caustic wit.

HÉRÉDIA, JOSE MARIA de (1842-1906). French poet, member of the group of Parnassian poets. He was born in Cuba but lived in France. His sonnets form a collection entitled *Les Trophées*.

HUGO, VICTOR MARIE (1802-1885). French poet, novelist, and dramatist In the dramas, *Hernani* (1830) and *Ruy Blas* (1838), he broke through the classical restrictions. In his lyric poetry, *Les feuilles d'automne* (1840) and *Contemplations* (1865), he invented or restored innumerable beauties of meter and harmony. He also wrote epic and satiric poetry. He wrote the novels *Notre Dame de Paris* (1831) and *Les Misérables* (1862) and thus influenced Romantic fiction throughout Europe.

IBROVAC, MIODRAG (1885-1973), Literary historian who wrote a number of studies and essays in Yugoslav and Western periodicals. His doctoral dissertation at the Sorbonne was on J. M. de Hérédia (Paris, 1923). At the University of Belgrade, he was a professor of French language and literature. He also edited the literary review, *Strani pregled* (The Foreign Review).

ILIĆ, DRAGUTIN (1858-1926). Serbian novelist, poet, and journalist. The son of Jovan Ilić, *q.v.*, his poems are not on the level of his brother Vojislav's, *q.v.*, poetry. His best works were his novels.

ILIĆ, JOVAN (1823-1901). Serbian poet and politician whose poetry was first influenced by classical poetry and later by the national epic poetry. His four sons, Dragutin, Vojislav, Milutin, and Žarko, were all involved in literature. His home was a gathering place for authors, poets, and novelists of the time. He was a cabinet member and a member of the Council of the State (Državni Savet).

ILIĆ, VOJISLAV (1860-1894). Serbian neoclassical poet, whose father and three brothers were poets and novelists. His literary development was influenced by Pushkin. His poems are elegant, somewhat restrained and pessimistic, with a deep feeling for nature. He brought new expression to Serbian poetry, and by the end of the nineteenth century, his influence on Serbian literature was the most absolute. (See Vojislavism).

ILLYRIAN MOVEMENT (ILLYRISM, ILIRSKI POKRET). Croatian cultural and national movement in 1830 through 1850, formed under the influence of the pan-slavic ideals of the period, as a reaction to the Austro-Hungarian cultural and intellectual oppression. The primary goal of the movement was a cultural and then eventually a political unification of the Southern Slavs. The leader of the movement was the Croatian poet, Ljudevit Gaj. Among other achievements, the Illyrian movement established the official literary language in Croatia, which was the same dialect already used by the reformer of the Serbian language, Vuk Stefanović Karađžić, *q.v.*

JANKOVIĆ, VLADIMIR-VELMAR (1895-?). Serbian writer who published a number of stories and plays.

JELIĆ, MILOSAV (1883-?). Army officer and poet whose patriotic poetry glorifying Serbian heroes throughout history was published in the collection, *Srbijanski Venac*.

JOVANOVIĆ, JOVAN-ZMAJ (1833-1904). Serbian lyric poet and the founder of Serbian children's literature, Jovanović was also a medical doctor. He published the journals, *Javor* and *Zmaj*, as well as *Neven*, which was the first Serbian periodical designed for children. His poetry for the very young is still popular and in print. Zmaj's lyric poetry is sensitive and melancholy, reflecting his personal tragedies—the loss of his beloved wife and child. His patriotic poetry expresses the feelings of his generation. He also translated German and Hungarian poetry. He lived and worked in Novi-Sad (Vojvodina), then part of the Austro-Hungarian Empire.

JOVANOVIĆ, LJUBOMIR (LJUBA-PATAK) (1865-1928). Serbian politician and historian. A professor of history at Velika Škola (later renamed the University of Belgrade), he wrote a number of historical studies. He was also a prominent member of the Radical Party and during World War I was the Minister of the Interior.

JOVANOVIĆ, MILUTIN (1881-1935). Serbian writer, poet, and army officer. His best known works are his novels depicting army life.

JOVANOVIĆ, VOJISLAV-MARAMBO (1884-?). Writer and diplomat. He studied Serbian epic poetry and its impact on European Romanticism and incorporated these studies in his doctoral dissertation "*La Guzla de Prosper Mérimée*"(1911). He also edited a collection of epic poetry *Srpske narodne pesme* (Belgrade, 1922) and *Srpske narodne pripovetke* (Belgrade, 1925). He wrote a number of studies and essays and translated Ibsen and Voltaire.

JOVKIĆ, PROKA (1886-1915). (Pseudonym, NESTOR ŽUČNI). Serbian patriotic and socialist poet. In 1903, he came to the U. S. from his native Sentomaš in Hungary. Here he worked as a longshoreman, factory worker, typographer, and editor. He published two collections of poems with strong socialist trends. In 1911, with the help of J. Skerlić, he moved to Belgrade, where he finished high school and started his studies at the University. His third collection of patriotic and lyrical poems was published in Belgrade.

KARAĐŽIĆ, VUK STEFANOVIĆ (1787-1864). Reformer of literary language. Born in a Serbian village, he lived in Vienna most of his life where he came in contact with leading Slavic scholars and folklorists. Among his friends were J. W. Goethe, J. Grimm, L. Ranke, and Dubrovsky. He collected epic folk poetry from the country "gusla" players and singers, as well as folk tales and proverbs. His first collection of folk poetry appeared in 1814 and 1815. In 1818, with the philologist Jernej Kopitar, he published *Srpski Rječnik* (an etymological dictionary of Serbian terms) based on the language spoken by the people. In it, Karadžić introduced the reformed orthographic and phonetic Cyrillic alphabet, which in turn replaced the Old Church Slavic-Serbian (Slavianoserbski) language and writing. He was a very productive writer. He gave a historical account of the First and Second Serbian Uprisings (1804; 1815) and wrote short monographs on the individuals of the period. His collection of epic poetry is the best anthology of its kind (four volumes re-issued several times), while his *Life and Customs of the Serbian People*, published posthumously, is a rich ethnographic reference work. He also translated the New Testament into modern language. Vuk Karadžić exerted a powerful influence on the new generation of Serbian writers, who in turn help him to bring to life National Romanticism.

KIPLING, RUDYARD (1865-1936). English author of poems, short stories, and novels, including *Plain Tales from the Hills, The Jungle Book,* and *Kim*. His collected poems include *Barrack-Room Ballads*.

KNEŽEVIĆ, BOŽIDAR (1862-1905). Philosopher, scholar and university professor. He wrote a number of philosophical studies while his major work relates to the principles of history.

KOROLIJA, MIRKO (1886-1934). Croatian poet and dramatist. Born in Dalmatia, he was the director of the National Theater in Split and Sarajevo. His rich and flamboyant poetry was influenced by G. D'Annunzio. His *Zidanje Skadra* was a very successful historical drama and his novels depicting life in small Dalmatian towns are quite colorful.

KOSSOVO. The battlefield in Serbia where, on June 28, 1389, the army of the Ottoman Empire, led by Sultan Murad I, attacked the Serbian army, led by Prince Lazar. Both rulers lost their lives, while the Serbian Kingdom lost its independence to the Turks for almost five centuries. The Battle of Kossovo became the symbol of national suffering and pride, glorified in the Serbian epic poetry.

KOSTIĆ, LAZA (1841-1910). Poet and dramatist. Very active politically in the patriotic youth movements of the nineteenth century. He studied Shakespeare and translated some of his works, introducing iambic form into Serbian poetry.

KOVAČEVIĆ, LJUBOMIR (1848-1918). Historian and professor at Velika Škola (later renamed the University of Belgrade) who wrote a number of studies on Serbian medieval history.

KOZAČINSKI, EMANUEL. Eighteenth century Russian educator. In 1733, he came with a group of Russian teachers to Sremski Karlovci in Vojvodina, then a part of the Austro-Hungarian Monarchy. Karlovci was the seat of the Orthodox Archbishopric (Mitropolija) and the center of cultural and religious life of the Serbian people.

LASCARIS, MILHAILO (1903-1965). Greek historian, professor at the University of Thessaloniki. He wrote about the relationship between the Byzantine Empire and Serbian Kingdom.

LAZAREVIĆ, DJORDJE (1887-1914). Political figure in Bosnia, where he was judge in Tuzla. Elected a member in the Bosanski Sabor, he was arrested in the first days of World War I as a hostage. He disappeared one night; his death was never officially accounted for.

LILIENCRON, DETLEV Freiherr von (1844-1909). German lyric poet. An Impressionist in his color verse. He also wrote ballads, plays, and novels about army life with which, as an army officer, he was familiar.

LUKOVIĆ, STEVAN (1877-1902). Serbian poet and close friend of J. Skerlić. His pessimistic and lyrical poetry was strongly influenced by the French Symbolists.

MAETERLINCK, Cte, MAURICE (1864-1949). Belgian poet, dramatist, and essayist. His works include the plays *Pélléas et Mélisande* (1892), *L'oiseau bleu* (1908), and *La vie des abeilles* (1901). During World War I, he wrote *Les Ruines de la Guerre*.

MAGRE, MAURICE (1877-1942). French poet whose poetry relates to the mysteries of occultism and magic. His main works include "Les Lèvres et le Secret," and "La Porte du mystère."

MARKOVIĆ, DANICA (1879-1932). Serbian poet and lyricist. Her poems expressed her most sincere inner emotions.

MATAVULJ, SIMO (1852-1908). Novelist, professor and journalist. He lived and worked in Herzegovina, Montenegro, and Serbia. His novels are pure realism describing life in Montenegro and Herzegovina with humor and light irony.

MAUPASSANT, GUY de (1850-1893). French writer, a master of the short story form, writing in a terse, naturalistic style. His stories include "Boule de Suif" (1880), "Mademoiselle Fifi" (1882), etc. Among his novels are *Une Vie* (1883), and *Bel Ami* (1885).

MAŽURANIĆ, IVAN (1814-1890). Croatian poet and "ban" of Croatia from 1873-1880. In his youth, Mažuranić belonged to the Illyrian Movement; however, later in life, as chief of the highest ranking office in Croatia, he supported the political interests of the Austro-Hungarian Empire. His principal literary work, *Smrt Smail Age Čengića* (1846), an epic, is among the most important literary works of Croatian poetry.

MEŠTROVIĆ, IVAN (1883-1962). Croatian sculptor. At the International Exhibition at Rome in 1911, he exhibited in the pavillion of the Kingdom of Serbia. His colossal sculptures commemorating the battle of Kossovo, and his model for the temple of Kossovo won him international recognition. Today, most of these sculptures are in the National Museum of Belgrade. His works are also found in major museums of other countries. He made several mausolea in Yugoslavia, and the two equestrian statues of Indians in Chicago. After World War II, he moved to the United States where he taught at Syracuse and Notre Dame universities, where he died in 1962.

MILAČIĆ, Dr. DUŠAN (1892-). Literary critic and historian. He was the director of the National Theatre and, after World War II, chief librarian of the National Library in Belgrade. He wrote a number of studies and essays on French literature.

MILIČIĆ, JOSIP SIBE (1886-). Yugoslav poet and diplomat. Born in Dalmatia, he moved to Belgrade in 1913. He wrote lyric poetry and novels with nostalgic overtones and mysticism.

MILOJEVIĆ, Dr. MILOJE (1884-). Serbian composer who also wrote essays on the theory of music and criticism. His numerous compositions are both orchestral and piano works as well as "Lieder."

MILUTIN (STEPHEN UROŠ I MILUTIN, 1282-1331). Serbian king. Milutin greatly expanded the territories of the Serbian medieval kingdom and built many churches and monasteries including a monastery in Jerusalem. His fourth wife was the Byzantine princess, Simonida, still a minor when he married her..

MITROVIĆ, MILORAD (1866-1907). Serbian poet. In his early years, he was greatly influenced by V. Ilić; but later developed his own style. He also wrote political fables and epigrams.

MUSSET, ALFRED de (1810-1857). French Romantic writer. His poems include *Les Nuits* (1835-37). His autobiographical novel, *La Confession d'un enfant du siècle* (1836), reveals attitudes and difficulties of his generation. His witty, delicate plays are published under the general title, *Comédies et proverbes*.

NAPRED (EN AVANT). *A newspaper, published in Tunis and Bizerta (Tunisia) from 1916 -1918* for the wounded and sick Serbian soldiers and refugees. It also had a literary supplement.

NIKOLAJEVIĆ, Dr. BOŽIDAR (1877-1947). Art historian, diplomat and writer. he wrote lyrical poetry, dramas, political essays and studies in the field of art history.

NJEGOŠ, PETAR II. (1830-1851). Poet, bishop and ruler of Montenegro. The greatest Serbian philosopher and writer of epic poetry. His principle work, *Gorski Vijenac*, was translated into ten languages. The English edition, P.P. Njegoš, *The Mountain Wreath*, was translated by James W. Wiles, London, in 1930. In the Introduction (p. 11, English Edition) V. Popović states: "What Shakespeare is to England, Njegoš is to Serbia."

NOVA ISKRA . Literary journal, published in Belgrade from 1899-1912. Publisher and editor was Rista Odavić.

NOVAKOVIĆ, BOŠKO (1905-). Modern Yugoslav literary historian and critic, professor at the University of Novi Sad.

NOVINE SRPSKE (or *SRPSKE NOVINE*). Serbian official gazette established in 1835, publishing all ordinances, laws, and decrees. During the exile of the Serbian government from 1916-1918, it was published in Corfu. In 1919, it was superceded by *Sluzbene Novine*.

NUŠIĆ, BRANISLAV (1864-1938). Leading Serbian dramatist who wrote over 30 plays, the best known of which are his satirical comedies. He also wrote some poems in his youth, as well as stories and travelogues.

ODAVIĆ, RISTA (1879-1932). Serbian lyric poet and dramatist. He published and edited the literary journal, *Nova Iskra, q.v.*, (1899-1907; 1911). He also translated Russian and German poetry.

PANDUROVIĆ, SIMA (1883-1960). Serbian poet and literary critic. Pandurović wrote poems, essays, and studies on literature; he was the founder of the literary magazine, *Misao* (1919). His poetry is very pessimistic.

PARNASSIANS (PARNASSIENS). Poets of the French Parnassian School during the second half of the nineteenth century. Their name was derived from the collection, *Le Parnasse Contemporain.* They strove toward perfection of form, erudition, and objectivity. The "l'art pour l'art" idea was formulated and realized in this school, and the Symbolist Movement reacted to the Parnassian analytic poetry. The Parnassians included Théophile Gauthier, Leconte de Lisle, Theodore de Banville, Francois Copée, Jose Maria de Hérédia, Sully Prudhomme.

PAŠIĆ, NIKOLA (1845-1926). Statesman, leader of the Serbian Radical party. He was the Prime Minister of the kingdom of Serbia several times, but his most important term of office was his ministry from 1912 to the end of World War I. After the war, he represented the Kingdom of Serbs, Croats, and Slovenes at the Peace Treaty at Versailles and again became prime minister, serving until his death.

PAYEN, LOUIS (1875- ?). French poet and author of "Herode" and "Jason." Founder of the literary magazine *La Coupe* in 1898. Milutin Bojić read the Serbian translation of "Herode," published in *Nova Iskra*, January 1911.

PÉGUY, CHARLES (1873-1914). French poet and essayist. He professed a mystical, patriotic socialism which opposed both anticlerical socialism and right-wing Catholicism.

PETKOVIĆ, VLADIMIR-DIS (1880-1917). Serbian poet, whose work was imbued with great lyricism. He died aboard a torpedoed ship during World War I.

PETRONIJEVIĆ, BRANISLAV (1875-1954). Philosopher, mathematician, and paleontologist. He was a professor at the University of Belgrade. His works are well known in the Western European scholarly world.

PIJEMONT. Serbian daily newspaper. Semi-official instrument of the organization "Ujedinjenje ili Smrt," *q.v.*.(Crna ruka). Published from 1911 to 1915 in Belgrade. Its emphasis was strongly nationalistic. The first editor and publisher was Ljubomir Jovanović-Čupa followed by Branko Božović.

POPOVIĆ, BOGDAN (1863-1944). Serbian literary critic and historian. He was professor at the University of Belgrade from 1893-1934, where he established the chair of comparative literature. In 1901 he started publishing a literary journal *Srpski Knježni Glasnik* (*q.v.*), which had a decisive influence on the development of Serbian literature. He was the first in Serbia to start scholarly research on the theory of literature and to study literature as an art form. He compiled the Anthology of modern Serbian lyric poetry (*Antologija novije srpske lirike*) first published in Zagreb in 1911; unrevised to date, it is in its 13th edition (Belgrade 1971). As the literary critic, educator and the editor of the literary journal, B. Popović played a most important role in all aspects of cultural life in Serbia.

POPOVIĆ, PAVLE ,(1868-1939). University professor, brother of Bogdan Popović (*q.v.*),. He wrote a number of historical and critical essays and studies in the field of Serbian literature.

POPOVIĆ-DEVEČERSKI, ZARIJE (1856-1934). Novelist who wrote a number of stories about the life of the Serbs under Turkish occupation in the nineteenth century.

PUTNIK, RADOMIR (1847-1917). Field Marshall of the Serbian army during the Balkan Wars (1912-1913) and in World War I. He was the Chief of Staff until the retreat of 1916.

RADIČEVIĆ, BRANKO (1824-1853). Serbian Romantic poet. He was the first to use the reformed Serbian literary language, thus starting the Serbian poetry of modern times. (See also KARADŽIĆ, VUK).

RAJIĆ, JOVAN (1726-1801). Monk and historian who wrote the first history of the southern Slavs (including Bulgarians) based on the study of archival material. His work greatly influenced nineteenth century historians.

RAJIĆ, VELIMIR (1879-1915). Serbian poet whose poetry is very personal, warm and melancholy.

RAKIĆ, MILAN (1876-1938). Serbian poet and diplomat, member of the Royal Academy of Sciences (Srpska Kraljevska Akademija Nauka). His poetry was influenced by the French Parnassians, but nevertheless remained individualistic in its noble style. He and Jovan Dučić, *q.v.*, were the greatest Serbian poets of the first four decades of the twentieth century.

RANKOVIĆ, SVETOLIK (1863-1899). Serbian Realist novelist. His literary formation was at first influenced by Russian Realism and later by the French Naturalist school. He was one of the leaders of the genre in the nineteenth century.

REVUE DES DEUX-MONDES. Bi-monthly French literary journal, founded in 1829, that greatly influenced French literature for over a century.

RIMBAUD, ARTHUR (1854-1891). French poet whose literary works, including "Le Bateau Ivre" (1871), "Les Illuminations" (published in 1886), and "Une Saison en Enfer" (1873), were all written before he was twenty. His poetry evolved from, as he said, a systematic transformation of the function of the senses and a naturally oblique expression.

ROMANTICISM. Term applied to the literary movement in the late eighteenth and in the nineteenth century. The basic aims of Romanticism were diverse: a return to nature and belief in the goodness of man, the rediscovery of the artist as a supremely individual creator and most of all, the exaltation of emotions over reason.

ROSSETTI, DANTE GABRIEL (GABRIEL CHARLES DANTE, 1882-1882). English poet and painter. With Millais and Holman Hunt, he formed the pre-Raphaeliste Brotherhood. With its passionate feeling, its sense of color and its preoccupation with medieval themes and atmosphere, his poetry creates a dream world of a group of artists who have turned away from society.

ROSTAND, EDMOND (1868-1918). French playwright. *Cyrano de Bergerac* (1897) and *L'Aiglon* (1900), his best known works, are distinguished by their wit and brilliance.

SAINT-SIMON, LOUIS de ROUVROY, duc de (1675-1755). French courtier and writer. His *Mémoires* provide a penetrating description of the French court from 1691 to 1723.

SAMAIN, ALBERT (1859-1900). French poet of the Symbolist school. He published *Au jardin de l'Infante* (1893) and *Aux flancs du vase* (1898). He was greatly influenced by Charles Baudelaire and Verlaine, but wrote more intimate poetry than either of them. He was the founder of the literary periodical, *Mercure de France*.

ŠANTIĆ, ALEKSA (1868-1924). Serbian poet from Mostar (Herzegovina). He wrote a number of patriotic and nationalistic poems, as well as very warm, lyrical poetry.

SATANISM-SATANIC SCHOOL. The name given to a group of French and English writers of the first half of the nineteenth century (Georges Sand, Victor Hugo, de Kock, Byron, Shelley, Moore) for their scorn for moral rules.

SCARLATTI, DOMENICO (1685-1757). Italian composer who wrote over 550 harpsichord "sonatas," single movement works in binary form, often characterized by harmonic and rhythmic variety and brilliance.

SCHILLER, JOHAN CHRISTOPH FREIDRICH VON (1759-1805). German poet, playwright, historian, and critic, who achieved instant fame with his Romantic drama, *Die Räuber* (1781). His historical dramas, *Maria Stuart* (1800) and *Wilhelm Tell* (1804), treat the themes of freedom, idealism, and heroic achievement. The same idealism is found in the poem, "The Hymn to Joy," which Beethoven set to music in the last movement of the Ninth Symphony.

SKARDALIJA. A section of Belgrade famous in the nineteenth century for several cafés which in turn were identified with the Bohemian style of life of the artists. Today, Skadarlija is restored as a tourist attraction.

SKERLIĆ, JOVAN (1877-1914). Leading literary critic and historian, professor of Serbian literature at the University of Belgrade from 1905 to 1914. His book, *The History of Modern Serbian Literature* (Istorija nove srpske književnosti, second edition, Belgrade, 1921), is still the basic work in the field. As the editor of *Srpski Književni Glasnik* (1905-1914), he had great influence upon young poets and writers.

SREMAC, STEVAN (1855-1906). Novelist, satirist, and humorist, and high school teacher in several small towns. His novels deal with folklore and local color. His main works are *Pop Ćira* and *Pop Spira, Ivkova Slava*, and *Zona Zamfirova*.

"SRPSKA KNJIŽEVNA ZADRUGA" (SKZ). Serbian literary cooperative, founded in 1892 in Belgrade. Its goal was to educate the taste of the readers and to publish works of Serbian authors. It also published translations of the best literary works throughout the ages. SKZ is still publishing, although its scope is changed.

SRPSKE NOVINE. See *Novine Srpske*.

SRPSKI KNJIŽEVNI GLASNIK. Bi-monthly literary journal founded in 1901 by B. Popović, *q.v.*, and published until 1941. It exerted a great deal of influence upon the generation of authors and poets of the first four decades of the century.

STANIMIROVIĆ, VLADIMIR (1882- ?). Serbian poet whose style was warm and direct, and whose poem about the Albanian Exodus (1915), *q.v.*, was dramatized.

STANKOVIĆ, BORISAV (1886-1927). Serbian writer and playwright. His theater play *Koštana*, as well as his famous novel *Nečista Krv*, deal with life in Vranje, and the novel is one of the best in Serbian modern literature.

STEFANOVIĆ, SVETISLAV (1874-1944). Serbian poet and medical doctor. He was quite familiar with English poetry and translated some of Shakespeare's works into Serbian. He also published novels and theater plays.

STERIJA POPOVIĆ, JOVAN (1806-1856). Serbian dramatist and novelist born in Vršac (Vojvodina), who wrote historical novels and plays, but his best works were social comedies, some of which are still performed.

SYMBOLISM. French school of the end of the nineteenth century which aimed at evoking moods that escape analysis rather than depicting emotions. The Symbolist school was a reaction against the Parnassian poetry which was based on a logical transcription of ideas. Symbolist poets brought poetry very close to music. Charles Baudelaire was a precursor of the school. Its leader was Stéphane Mallarmé and its main representative was Paul Verlaine. Other Symbolist poets were Henri de Regnier, Jean Moréas, Maurice Maeterlinck, Gustave Kahn, Jules Laforgues, and Albert Samain.

TAINE, HYPPOLITE (1828-1893). French philosopher, literary critic and historian. He applied theories of determinism to literary criticism, aesthetics, and psychology. His best known work is *Origines de la France contemporaine* (1875-1893).

TRIFKOVIĆ, KOSTA (1843-1873). Serbian dramatist. Living in Novi Sad at the time of the Austro-Hungarian Empire, he wrote amusing comedies, as well as some poems and novels.

TRIFKOVIĆ, MARKO (1864-1928). Politician and member of Pasić's Radical party. He was elected to the Parliament several times and also served as Minister a number of times.

"UJEDINJENJE ILI SMRT" (UNIFICATION OR DEATH). Also known as "Crna Ruka" (Black Hand). Secret nationalist organization formed by army officers in the spring of 1911. The goal was, as indicated by the name, either the unification of all the territories inhabited by Serbs, or the death of the members of the movement. At the time, some territories of the medieval Serbian kingdom were still under Turkish domination. Vojvodina (Srem, Banat, Bačka) was under Hungarian rule as part of the Austro-Hungarian Empire, while Bosnia and Herzegovina had just been annexed by Austria in 1908. In 1914, preceding the declaration of war, the Austro-Hungarian government accused some of the officers of this organization of being instrumental in the assassination of the Crown Prince Ferdinand on June 28, 1914, in Sarajevo.

UROŠ THE WEAK (Emperor STEPHEN UROŠ, 1355-1371). Inherited his father's empire, but lacked his father's energy and authority needed to hold the vast estate together; thus, it disintegrated into a number of small principalities and despotates.

USKOKOVIĆ, MILUTIN (1884-1915). Writer and journalist. Received a doctor's degree in law from the University of Geneva in 1910. He wrote short stories and novels; best known are *Došljaci* and *Čedomir Ilić*. In 1915 he committed suicide when witnessing the tragedy of the Serbian retreat.

VENAC. Literary journal founded in 1910, especially oriented toward high school students. It published contributions of established authors as well as those of beginners, thus encouraging young people to write.

VERHAEREN, EMILE (1855-1916). Belgian lyric poet of the French Symbolist school. During World War I, he published "La Belgique sanglante," and "Parmi les ruines."

VERLAINE, PAUL (1844-1896). French poet of the Symbolist school, with an intensely refined musical and rhythmic sense. His poems are highly sophisticated, yet cultivate a simplicity akin to folk poetry. His poems were put to music by a great number of French composers, especially Fauré.

VESELINOVIĆ, JANKO (1862-1905). Serbian novelist. As a young school teacher, he spent years in villages and wrote a number of stories idealizing village and country life.

VIDO. Small island in the Ionian Sea, close to Corfu. In 1916, soldiers, ill and exhausted from crossing the Albanian Mountains, were transferred to Vido. Because a great number of them died, the island was also known as the "Island of Death," and the open sea into which the bodies were lowered was called "the blue grave."

VIGNY, ALFRED de (1797-1863). French poet, playwright, and novelist. One of the leaders of the Romantic school. Besides lyric poetry such as "Poèmes antiques et modernes" (1826) and "Les Destinées" (1864), he wrote novels including *Cinq-Mars* (1826), and dramas, including *Chatterton* (1835).

VINAVER, STANISLAV (1891-1955). Serbian poet, literary critic, and journalist who was well known for his parodies on the contemporary poetry and for the high quality of his translations (Rabelais).

VOJISLAVISM. Movement in Serbian poetry during the nineteenth century named after the poet, Vojislav Ilić. The influence of this style was particularly strong during the last decade of the century.

VOJNOVIĆ, IVO (1857-1929). Nobleman and writer from Dubrovnik. He was first influenced by the French Realist school, but eventually turned to the Symbolist style. He was best known for his dramatic work. Some of his plays are patriotic, such as *Smrt Majke Jugovića*, inspired by the heroism of the Serbian army in the Balkan Wars. *Dubrovačka Trilogija* is his most powerful dramatic work.

VUJIĆ, JOAKIM (1722-1847). Dramatist and originator of the first theater in nineteenth century Serbia, who also wrote of his travels and gave a description of Serbia of the time.

WELLS, H. GEORGE (1866-1946). English novelist and journalist, Wells is known for his science fiction and his satirical novels. He also wrote a popular *Outline of History*, (1920).

WILDE, OSCAR (1854-1900). Irish writer, playwright, and wit. His play, *Salome* differs greatly from his other witty plays, *e.g.*, *The Importance of Being Earnest*. Wilde is also known for his novel, *The Picture of Dorian Grey*, and his long poem, *The Ballad of Reading Gaol*, composed after his imprisonment.

WORLD WAR I – SERBIA. On August 11, 1914, the Austro-Hungarian Empire attacked the kingdom of Serbia following the assassination of Crown Prince Ferdinand in Sarajevo on June 28, 1914. During the summer and fall of 1914, the Serbian army defeated the numerically larger and technically better-equipped Austro-Hungarian troops. It was only in 1915, when German Field Marshall General von Mackensen organized a massive offensive against Serbia from the west, north, and east (Bulgaria had entered the war on the side of the Central Powers–Germany and Austro-Hungary), that the Serbian army could no longer resist. The only possible way of escape was the snow- and ice-covered mountains of the south-west, generally considered insurmountable. Thus began the Albanian Exodus *q.v.* In the spring of 1916, while the exiled Serbian government was at Corfu, the Serbian troops rested and re-organized, and then were sent to the Thessaloniki front where they fought all the battles with the Allied Armies. Fighting and liberating their country foot by foot, Serbian soldiers made their way north to Belgrade, which they entered triumphantly on Nov. 1. 1918. On December 1, 1918, the kingdom of Serbs, Croats, and Slovenes was officially proclaimed. This new state united the kingdoms of Serbia and Montenegro, and the former territories of the Austro-Hungarian Empire–Slovenia, Croatia, Dalmatia, Vojvodina, and Bosnia and Herzegovina (annexed by Austria in 1908). Later, in 1929, the name of the kingdom was officially changed to the Kingdom of Yugoslavia.

ZABAVNIK. Supplement to *Novine Srpske, q.v.* Started at Corfu in 1917, it focussed on the literary works of exiled writers.

ZEČEVIĆ, MILOŠ (1838-1896). Historian and professor of history at the Velika Skola (later renamed the University of Belgrade). His major work, *Istorija sveta* (History of the World), although not on a scholarly level, had great influence on the youth of Serbia.

ZEJTINLIK. Military cemetery near Thessaloniki, where Serbian and French soldiers were buried during World War I.

ŽIVADINOVIĆ, STOJAN (1890-1942). Serbian writer and diplomat, who wrote stories and novels, some of which are from Serbian history.

ŽIVANOVIĆ, JEREMIJA (1874-1940). Professor who, in 1910, founded the literary journal *Venac*. After World War I, he established and was co-editor of the voluminous series *Biblioteka srpskih pisaca* (The Library of Serbian Authors).

ZOLA, EMILE (1840-1902). French novelist and leading exponent of Naturalism. In his twenty-volume *Rougon-Macquart* series (1869-93), he traces the family's history as a result of social and natural laws. His best known novels are *L'Assomoir* (1877) and *Germinal* (1885).

ZORA. Literary journal. From 1896-1901, it was published monthly in Mostar (Herzegovina) by a group of Serbian authors and poets such as A. Šantić, S. Ćorović, and J. Dučić. Mostar was the Serbian cultural and literary center of the territories under the Austro-Hungarian Empire.

EAST EUROPEAN MONOGRAPHS

1. *Political Ideas and the Enlightenment in the Romanian Principalities, 1750-1831.* By Vlad Georgescu. 1971.
2. *America, Italy and the Birth of Yugoslavia, 1917-1919.* By Dragan R. Zivojinovic. 1972.
3. *Jewish Nobles and Geniuses in Modern Hungary.* By William O. McCagg, Jr. 1972.
4. *Mixail Soloxov in Yugoslavia: Reception and Literary Impact.* By Robert F. Price. 1973.
5. *The Historical and National Thought of Nicolae Iorga.* By William O. Oldson. 1973.
6. *Guide to Polish Libraries and Archives.* By Richard C. Lewanski. 1974.
7. *Vienna Broadcasts to Slovakia, 1938-1939: A Case Study in Subversion.* By Henry Delfiner. 1974.
8. *The 1917 Revolution in Latvia.* By Andrew Ezergailis. 1974.
9. *The Ukraine in the United Nations Organization: A Study in Soviet Foreign Policy. 1944-1950.* By Konstantin Sawczuk. 1975.
10. *The Bosnian Church: A New Interpretation.* By John V.A. Fine, Jr. 1975.
11. *Intellectual and Social Developments in the Habsburg Empire from Maria Theresa to World War I.* Edited by Stanley B. Winters and Joseph Held. 1975.
12. *Ljudevit Gaj and the Illyrian Movment.* By Elinor Murray Despalatovic. 1975.
13. *Tolerance and Movements of Religious Dissent in Eastern Europe.* Edited by Bela K. Kiraly. 1975.
14. *The Parish Republic: Hlinka's Slovak People's Party, 1939-1945.* By Yeshayahu Jelinek. 1976.
15. *The Russian Annexation of Bessarabia, 1774-1828.* By George F. Jewsbury. 1976.
16. *Modern Hungarian Historiography.* By Steven Bela Vardy. 1976.
17. *Values and Community in Multi-National Yugoslavia.* By Gary K. Bertsch. 1976.
18. *The Greek Socialist Movement and the First World War: the Road to Unity.* By George B. Leon. 1976.
19. *The Radical Left in the Hungarian Revolution of 1848.* By Laszlo Deme. 1976.
20. *Hungary between Wilson and Lenin: The Hungarian Revolution of 1918-1919 and the Big Three.* By Peter Pastor. 1976.
21. *The Crises of France's East-Central European Diplomacy, 1933-1938;.* By Anthony J. Komjathy. 1976.
22. *Polish Politics and National Reform, 1775-1788;* By Daniel Stone. 1976.
23. *The Habsburg Empire in World War I.* Robert A. Kann, Bela K. Kiraly, and Paula S. Fichtner, eds. 1977.
24. *The Slovenes and Yugoslavism, 1890-1914.* By Carole Rogel. 1977.
25. *German-Hungarian Relations and the Swabian Problem.* By Thomas Spira. 1977.
26. *The Metamorphosis of a Social Class in Hungary During the Reign of Young Franz Joseph.* By Peter I. Hidas. 1977.
27. *Tax Reform in Eighteenth Century Lombardy.* By Daniel M. Klang. 1977.
28. *Tradition versus Revolution: Russia and the Balkans in 1917.* By Robert H. Johnston. 1977.
29. *Winter into Spring: The Czechoslovak Press and the Reform Movement 1963-1968.* By Frank L. Kaplan. 1977.
30. *The Catholic Church and the Soviet Government, 1939-1949.* By Dennis J. Dunn. 1977.
31. *The Hungarian Labor Service System, 1939-1945.* By Randolph L. Braham. 1977.
32. *Consciousness and History: Nationalist Critics of Greek Society 1897-1914.* By Gerasimos Augustinos. 1977.
33. *Emigration in Polish Social and Political Thought, 1870-1914.* By Benjamin P. Murdzek. 1977.

34 *Serbian Poetry and Milutin Bojić.* By Mihailo Dordevic. 1977.

UNIVERSITY LIBRARY NOTTINGHAM